Dare to Be

A Devotional for Teen Girls

ISBN: 978-1-7351245-0-6
ISBN: 978-1-7351245-1-3
Library of Congress Control Number: 2020913428

Portions of this book are works of nonfiction. Certain names and identifying characteristics have been changed.

Printed in the United States of America.

First printing, 2020.

Jamie Kirschner
705 Berkshire Drive
Old Hickory, TN 37138

www.uncommonteen.com

Table of Contents

Part 3: Dare to Lead..........................99

Thank You..................................151

Part 1:
Dare to Be…
Beautiful

Day 1: Dare to Be Beautiful

Charm is deceitful and beauty is passing, but a woman who fears the Lord, she shall be praised.
Proverbs 31:30

WORD STUDY
FEAR: Hebrew Word: yârê

When we read this word fear, many times we think, "Afraid" or "Scared," however, many times when we read this word in the Old Testament, it actually means, "To put God first." We could actually read this verse like this: "Charm is deceitful and beauty is passing, but a woman who puts God first in her life, she shall be praised."

DEVOTIONAL

Have you ever heard the quote, "We are our own worst critic?" There is so much truth to that statement! So many times, as girls, we tend to beat ourselves up over everything...our hair, our skin, our weight, our personality, even our laugh.

We can be so quick to point out all of our "flaws." Maybe we think our noses are too big (this was so me!) and we wish it could be smaller; or maybe we are short, and we would like to be taller; or maybe we are quiet, and we wish we could be bubblier and more outgoing. It seems like there is always something, right?

If I were to ask you to list 10 things about yourself that you wish you could change, I can almost guarantee each one of us could come up with them pretty easily. But...if I were to ask you to come up with 10 things about yourself that you love and would never want to change, would it be that easy? Not for most of us.

Proverbs 31:30 tells us that charm is deceitful, and beauty is passing, but a woman who [puts God first], she shall be praised.

We've all met those charming people. They seem to just draw the crowds. However, just because someone is charming and a lot of people are looking up to them, it doesn't mean that we should be following them as well. Charm can be deceitful, especially if the person who is charming doesn't have great morals or doesn't make the best choices. On the surface, it can seem great, but eventually that charm can hurt many people.

For example, we have all met those girls that we think are just naturally beautiful. Like, "it's not fair" beautiful. I'm not talking about inner beauty here; I'm talking about their appearance…their looks. People tend to draw close to people who seem to "have it all together" on the outside, but that doesn't mean that they "have it all together" on the inside.

But what does someone look like who does "have it all together on the inside," someone who isn't just beautiful on the outside, but they are beautiful on the inside? How do we make sure that we are not just beautiful on the outside, but beautiful on the inside, too?

The only way that we can be sure that we are beautiful on the inside is to put God first in our lives. When we put God first in our lives, He is able to take those areas that may not look so beautiful and begin to transform them into areas that are completely healed and beautiful.

CONNECT
God doesn't want us to be afraid of Him, but He does want us to put Him first, because, since He created us, He knows how we function best. He knows that when we put Him first, our life will be the most blessed. Take time today to talk to God about the areas that you are holding back from Him.

Ask Him to help you put Him first in those areas. He wants to help you! When you pray, pray in faith without doubting. When you end your prayer, say, "I believe it and receive it in Jesus' Name." Then choose to believe it and receive it.

TAKE ACTION

Below, write down how this new definition of fear (to put God first) has help you see God differently? What is one area of your life you have been holding back from Him, maybe an area you are struggling with? What is one thing you can do today to put God first in that one area?

_____

_____

_____

_____

_____

_____

_____

_____

_____

_____

_____

_____

_____

_____

PRAY THE WORD

Thank You, Lord, that Proverbs 31:10, as I put you first in my life above everything else, You are making me truly beautiful.

Day 2: Media's Influence on Beauty

And do not be conformed to this world, but be transformed
by the renewing of your mind that you may prove what is that
good, and acceptable and perfect will of God.
Romans 12:2

WORD STUDY
Conform: Greek Word: suschēmatizō

Conforming to the outer appearance of this world's system.

DEVOTIONAL

If I were to ask you who you think is the most beautiful girl alive is, who would you say? Who is the very first person that came to mind? Was it some famous person? Was it someone that you follow on social media? Or, was it someone like your mom, your grandma or your best friend?

For most of us, it wasn't our mom, our grandma or our best friend that came to mind, but rather someone who is either famous or that we follow on social media. They are usually the ones who seem to be the "perfect" size, have the "perfect" skin, and have the "perfect" hair. If we are honest with ourselves, these are girls we secretly wish we could be.

Sometimes, when we look at pictures of these girls on social media or in movies, we start to feel bad about ourselves, because we don't look like they do. Maybe we aren't a size 0; maybe we have pimples or freckles on our face; maybe our nose is a little bit wide or too narrow. Before we realize it, that person who we think is beautiful, makes us feel terrible.

The truth is, media really can affect the way we see ourselves. We begin to compare who we are and what we look like with someone else and in many cases, we've never seen in real life. The problem with that is...most of what we see on social media is fake. I can assure you that most of the pictures we see of celebrity teens who post on social media have been altered or airbrushed to be something that they really aren't. Yes, even celebrity teens have pimples and freckles and are not necessarily a size 0!

The way we see ourselves is a direct reflection of our thoughts about ourselves. I want to encourage you, though. The more you understand how much God loves you and how incredibly beautiful He created you to be, the more you will begin to like who you really are. That is where our focus should be. Who God created you to be.

CONNECT

Is there something about yourself that you nitpick? Something about yourself that you constantly tear apart. Talk to God about this area of your life. God created you so beautifully and wants to help you learn to like yourself just the way you are. When you pray, be sure to pray in faith without doubting. When you end your prayer, say, "I believe it and receive it in Jesus' Name." Then choose to believe it and receive it.

TAKE ACTION

Romans 12:2 tells us to not be conformed to the patterns of this world, but to be transformed by the renewing of our minds. In order to do this, we need to begin to change what we are putting inside of us.

I want to encourage you today, when these thoughts come up in your mind about you not being good enough or that you aren't perfect, change those thoughts. Instead of constantly thinking about them all of the time, choose to say, "No more! I am beautiful just the way God made me!"

Write down below, "I am beautiful. I am beautiful just the way I am. I am beautiful just how God made me. I am beautiful!"

_____

_____

_____

_____

_____

_____

_____

_____

_____

_____

_____

_____

_____

_____

_____

_____

_____

_____

_____

PRAY THE WORD

Thank You, Lord that Romans 12:2, instead of comparing myself to this world's standards of beauty, I am choosing to be transformed by renewing my mind to what God says about me: I am beautiful!

Day 3: The Comparison Trap

For we dare not class ourselves or compare ourselves with those who commend themselves; But they, measuring themselves by themselves, and comparing themselves among themselves, are not wise.
2 Corinthians 10:12

DEVOTIONAL

Okay, so I know that I am not the only one who has ever done this. Have you ever walked into a room, saw another girl and then began to compare yourself to her? I don't mean from a, "Who does she think she is?" or an "I'm better than you attitude," but from an "I wish I was ____ like her" attitude.

For example, "I wish I was thin like her. She doesn't even have to try;" or "She is naturally beautiful, I wish I could look more like her;" or even, "It's so easy for her to make friends. Why can't I make friends like that?"

If we aren't careful, we can get stuck in what is called, "The Comparison Trap" and it is not a good place to be. Actually, being stuck in the comparison trap can be a very dangerous place to be. Dangerous? Really? Yes, because instead of seeing ourselves as the incredibly beautiful creation that God made us to be, we begin to wish we were someone else...someone God never intended for us to be. When we start comparing ourselves with others, we can begin to start dressing like them, acting like them and looking like them in order to be like them. When we try to become someone that we're not, we will end up losing who it is that God truly made us to be.

And the biggest problem of all is that once we have stepped into the trap of comparison, it's hard to break free. If we don't take action against it when we are young, it follows us throughout the rest of our lives. I have seen grown women, like even grandmas who still struggle with comparison.

This was something as a teen that I struggled with so much. I was not from a family who had a lot of money. I didn't have the nicest clothes or the newest trends and I hated it. I remember one time staying the night at my grandma's house and I didn't have clothes to wear to school the next day. I had to wear some of her clothes she had laying around. It was embarrassing! I was constantly comparing myself to everyone around me.   Because of getting stuck in the comparison trap during my teen years, I completely lost who I was as a person. It wasn't until I was in college that God began to work in me to show me who I was created to be.

Instead of comparing ourselves to other girls. Why don't we start comparing ourselves to our own potential? Why not change the question, "How can I be more like her?" To "How can I become a better me?"

This makes me think of David right before he went to fight Goliath. David was a young teen at the time. He was not a trained warrior, but a shepherd who knew that with God He could do anything...and this shepherd boy had just talked King Saul into letting him go and fight a giant. In 1 Samuel 17:38 we see King Saul trying to dress David in his own armor. There was a problem, though, King Saul was a grown man who had been wearing armor for quite some time, David was not. Once David had the helmet on his head, and had his sword fastened in, he tried walking around and he couldn't even move. Verse 39 tells us that David wasn't used to wearing all that weight. That was not who he was.

King Saul was trying to get David to be someone that he wasn't by having him wear his armor. David tried it out but knew that he couldn't do it. So, what did David do? He took off the armor, grabbed his staff, five smooth stones from the stream and his sling. Why? Because David was a shepherd. That was who he was and that was how he functioned best.

The same thing is true for you. Instead of asking, "How can I be more like her?" ask yourself, "How can I be a better me?"

CONNECT
Are you caught up in the comparison trap? Talk to God about helping you to see yourself as He sees you. When you pray, pray in faith without doubting. When you end your prayer, say, "I believe it and receive it in Jesus' Name." Then choose to believe it and receive it.

TAKE ACTION
Write below 3 things about yourself that make you who you are? How can you strengthen those areas to become a better you?

1. _____
_____
_____
_____
_____
_____
_____
_____
_____
_____

2. _____
_____
_____

3. _____

_____

_____

_____

_____

_____

_____

_____

_____

_____

_____

_____

_____

PRAY THE WORD

Thank You, Lord that 2 Corinthians 10:12, that I am choosing not to compare myself to others, but I am choosing to compare myself to my own potential, that I can become who it is that You created me to be.

Day 4: Combatting Media

If then you were raised with Christ, seek those things which are above, where Christ is, sitting at the right hand of God. Set your mind on things above, not on things on the earth.
Colossians 3:1-2

DEVOTIONAL

Did you know that advertisers spend over $500 billion a year marketing to youth alone? That's a lot of money to spend on targeting anyone, let alone youth. Why is it do you think they spend so much money on targeting teens? It's because they know that if they can target a teen's insecurities, they can get them (or their parents) to buy their products.

Think about it, we want to fit in. We want to look beautiful and wear clothes that are trendy or popular. We don't want to be thought of as an outcast. We want to be accepted by those who are around us. We want beautiful skin and beautiful hair. Did you know that God actually wired us with the need to be accepted? However, He wired us with the need to be accepted by Him, not to get our acceptance from those who are around us.

This makes me think back to the life of Daniel in Daniel 1 when he first went to Babylon. If you're not familiar with the story, I encourage you to read it. Did you know that Daniel was only 17 at the time he stood up to King Nebuchadnezzar?

You see, King Nebuchadnezzar had led the Babylonians to conquer Jerusalem. After Jerusalem was conquered, the king knew he needed help governing the new Babylon. In order to do this, he decided to choose young men from among the children of Israel. These were young men who were without blemish (clear skin) and who were thought of as good looking and strong. The young men that they chose had to be smart and had to be able to learn quickly. In other words, these young men were teenagers who had perfect skin, were good looking, were strong and were smart.

After the young men were chosen, Daniel 1:5-8 tells us that the king planned out all the food they were going to eat (junk food) and the wine that they were going to drink for three years. The king thought that if they changed their diet like this that these men would become strong enough to serve the king. However, Daniel chose not to give into the king. The Bible says that Daniel purposed in his heart that he would not defile himself with the king's junk food and wine.

The king didn't just stop with wanting to change these young men's diets, but actually the very first thing he did when they got to the palace was change their name. What the king was trying to do was change who they were. He didn't want them associating with Jerusalem any longer. He wanted to turn them into Babylonians, something they were not.

This is the very same tactic that marketers do today to reach teens. They try to reach deep into your identity and get to your insecurities. Once they have reached the part of you that they know they can touch, then they begin to change your "name" and your "diet."

This comes in the form of "You're ugly, so try this new product or wear these type of clothes;" or "You're fat, try this new diet or this new trend to help you lose weight;" or "You're an outcast, so try this new thing to help you fit in." The problem with this is that those things are not who you are! That is not who God created you to be. You are beautiful!

God says that you are beautiful. He says that you are accepted and loved! He chose you and adopted you into His family. I encourage you to read Ephesians 1 and 2 to help you see who God says you really are.

CONNECT

Ask God to help you see yourself as He created you to be. When you pray, pray in faith without doubting. When you end your prayer, say, "I believe it and receive it in Jesus' Name." Then choose to believe it and receive it.

TAKE ACTION

Who does God say you are? Look up these verses and write on the line next to them what God says about you.

Romans 8:37

_____

_____

_____

_____

2 Corinthians 5:17

_____

_____

_____

_____

Ephesians 1:4

_____

_____

_____

_____

Ephesians 1:5

_____

_____

_____

_____

Ephesians 1:6

_____

_____

_____

_____

2 Peter 2:9

_____

_____

_____

_____

Ephesians 2:10

_____

_____

_____

_____

PRAY THE WORD

Thank You, Lord, that Ephesians 1:3-6, my focus is on You and who you say I am. Lord, You call me blessed. You chose me before the foundation of the world. I am holy and blameless before You in love. It pleased You to adopt me as your daughter. I thank You, that I am accepted by You in love.

Day 5: Confidence Matters

Therefore do not cast away your confidence which has great reward.
Hebrews 10:35

WORD STUDY
CONFIDENCE: Greek Word: parrhēsia

Bold, free, openly bold

DEVOTIONAL

The more we see ourselves from God's point of view, the more confident we will become. Our confidence doesn't come from who we are or what we do, it comes from who God says we are and what Jesus has done for us.

When I think of someone who was confident, I think of Queen Esther. Stepping into being a queen as a teen, Esther was faced with a pretty big challenge that could have very well cost her life.

When Esther was 14 years old, she was chosen to be the next queen of Persia. About the same time that Esther was chosen to be queen, a man named Haman was given a promotion to become King Xerxes' right hand man. During his promotion, all of the servants who were within the king's gate all bowed down and paid respect to Haman...all except for one man named Mordecai.

Mordecai just so happened to be Esther's uncle and their family were Jews. Haman hated the Jewish people, so when he saw that Mordecai wasn't going to bow down and pay respect to Haman, Haman was furious. He wanted nothing more than to wipe all the Jews completely out of their country. So, Haman devised a plan to kill all of the Jews and had the king sign off on it.

What Haman didn't realize, though, was that King Xerxes' new queen, Esther, was a Jew also.

When Esther discovered this plot, she had two choices, not do anything about it and see all of the Jewish people, her family, destroyed or stand up and go to the king. That second option doesn't seem so bad unless you know the authority that kings carried back then. You see, in these days, the queen didn't have the right or authority to go see the king without her being summoned to him. If the queen went to the king and he did not expect to see her or want to see her, he would have her put to death immediately.

I don't know about you, but that's a pretty scary problem, especially for a teenage girl to face. However, Esther chose to be courageous. She knew what she had to do and she knew that she had the favor of God on her life. God had placed her in that palace for a purpose.

Where did Esther get the courage to stand up to the king like that? We see that when Esther became queen, she knew that it was God who placed her in that position, it had nothing to do with her, other than listening to God. So, when she was faced with that life or death decision, instead of jumping right in with her emotions, she took several days to get alone with God and pray. She wanted to make sure she was doing His will for her life.

When you're faced with a big challenge or a very stressful situation, what is your first go to? Is it your friends? Is it social media? Is it a book you like to lose yourself in? It is your parents or guardians? Or, like Esther, is it God? I encourage you, when you are faced with something big, go to God first and there you will find your courage! Then, find someone you can trust who has a strong relationship with God and have them stand with you on what you're believing for. There is strength in numbers. Esther didn't go to God alone, there were others that were praying and fasting with her during this time.

CONNECT

If there is a challenge that you are facing or a stressful situation, take time to talk to God and ask Him to help you through this time. He doesn't want you to be alone in this. When you pray, be sure to pray in faith without doubting. When you end your prayer, say, "I believe it and receive it in Jesus' Name." Then choose to believe it and receive it.

TAKE ACTION

When you're faced with a big challenge, what is your first go to? Is it your friends? It is your parents or guardians? Or is it God? Why do you think that is?

_____

_____

_____

_____

_____

_____

_____

_____

_____

_____

_____

_____

_____

PRAY THE WORD

Thank You, Lord, Hebrews 10:35, that because of You, I am holding onto my confidence and will not cast it away.

Day 6: True Beauty is Found in Jesus

She extends her hand to the poor, yes,
she reaches out her hands to the needy.
Proverbs 31:20

DEVOTIONAL

When I think of someone who is beautiful, I think of someone who has a loving, giving and caring heart. I think of someone who isn't selfish, but instead they are completely selfless.

Looking back at the life of Jesus, we see that He was someone who had such a beautiful heart. He was loving, giving and caring. When reading the Gospels (the books of Matthew, Mark, Luke and John), we get to see His true image and character. That is the same image and character of our Heavenly Dad. 1 John 4:8 tells us that God is love. He is the very essence of love!

Did you know that when Jesus was just 12 years old, He was already studying the Word of God in depth? He couldn't get enough of spending time with God. Reading the Word, He knew what was eventually going to happen to Him on the cross. He knew that He was going to be beaten beyond recognition, but He still chose to follow God anyway. Why?

Honestly, I can't say that if I was Jesus and I knew all that He was going to go through that I would still want to go through with it. Yet, Jesus chose to anyway! Praise God it was Jesus and not me! Why, though? Why did Jesus go to the cross when He had the power to stop what was going to happen by not following the will of God? It was because of His great love for us.

True beauty is found in Jesus, because of His selfless, unconditional love for us…and that is where our true beauty is found as well. The more time we spend with Him, the more we start acting like Him.

When we hang around someone, we will eventually start acting like them. For example, have you ever had that friend and they used the same phrase over and over again? They almost become infamous for it, right? When I was in college, I hung around a friend of mine whose favorite word was, "awesome." Everything was "awesome!" He said it so much that when people thought about him, they thought about that word. The more I began to hang around him with our group of friends, the more I caught myself using that word. We become like the people we hang around.

The more we hang out with Jesus, the more we become like Him. But in what ways can we become more like Jesus? I'm glad you asked!

1. We Encourage Others. Instead of judging others for things that they do, we choose to love them where they are, but encourage them to be all that God created them to be.

2. We Have Compassion on Others. Instead of just seeing a problem, we can start to think, "What can I do to help?" In Matthew 9:36, we see that Jesus was moved with compassion when he saw the crowd wandering aimlessly like sheep without a shepherd.

3. We Forgive Quickly. Know that just because you have forgiven someone who really hurt you, it doesn't mean that you have to trust them again quickly. Trust has to be earned.

4. We Love Others with the Love of Jesus. John 15:12-13 says, "This is my commandment, that you love one another as I have loved you. Greater love has no one that this, than to lay down one's life for his friends."

CONNECT
Take time to talk to God today about helping you to become more like Him. How can you be more encouraging, more compassionate, more forgiving and more loving? Remember, when you pray, pray in faith without doubting.

When you end your prayer, say, "I believe it and receive it in Jesus' Name." Then choose to believe it and receive it.

TAKE ACTION
Out of these 4 areas, encouraging others, having compassion on others, forgiving others and loving others. What one area could you improve in? What is one thing you can do today to help you take action?

_____

_____

_____

_____

_____

_____

_____

_____

_____

_____

_____

_____

_____

_____

PRAY THE WORD
I thank You, Lord, that just like in Proverbs 31:20, that I am focused on reaching out to those around me and blessing them. Thank You, Lord for helping me to become more like Jesus.

Day 7: True Beauty is Found in a Relationship with God

And this is eternal life, that they may know You,
the only true God, and Jesus Christ Whom You sent.
John 17:3

DEVOTIONAL

When I made Jesus the Lord of my life, I was an emotional mess. I had a lot of insecurities and built up a lot of walls from past abuse and hurt. I had a hard time trusting anyone. One thing I love about our God, though, is He reached out to me right where I was and completely changed my life. I went from a broken teenage girl to being adopted into my Heavenly Dad's family.

When we choose to make Jesus the Lord of our lives, 2 Corinthians 5:17 tells us that we instantly become a new creation in Christ. Our past is completely gone, and everything is made brand new. Thank You, Jesus!

I have heard so many people, once they become a Christian, say things like, "I'm religious" or "I've found religion." However, there is an incredible difference between religion and having a relationship with God. What is the difference between religion and a relationship? With religion, we have to try to do everything as best we can and then present it to a god saying, "I have done all these things right, will you accept it?" In a relationship with God, Jesus has done everything for us and then turns to us and says, "I have done all these things for you, will you accept it?"

Every single one of us is born with a God shaped hole in our hearts that must be filled. We try to fill that hole with many things—this can be sin or it can even be with good things that don't actually fulfill us. When we give our life to Jesus, He fills that hole inside of us. When He fills that hole, He takes our emptiness, our fear and our pain and fills us with joy, peace and love. A relationship with Jesus doesn't just change our actions to make sure that we are better people! It transforms us from the inside out.

If you are reading this and maybe you've gone to church your whole life, but you haven't actually entered into a relationship with Jesus...or you feel empty on the inside and you want to have that life-changing transformation like I had. A relationship with God is so simple to receive.

All you need to do is believe that Jesus came to this earth, died on the cross for your sins, was raised up from death to life by the power of God and now sits at the right hand of God. Then pray this prayer out loud, but most importantly mean it from your heart. It doesn't matter where you are or what you have done, God will meet you right there with His arms of love open wide waiting for you to come in.

Say this out loud:

> *"Father, I come to you now. Sin and Satan, I turn my back on you. Jesus, I turn to you now. I believe that you died on the cross for me. I believe that you were raised from the dead just for me. Come into my heart. Be my Lord. Today, I begin a brand new life with you. I am choosing to enter into that life-changing relationship with you today! I believe that Jesus is my Lord!"*

That's it! It's that simple! All you have to do is just accept all that God has done for you and now you have entered into a loving relationship with God! If you prayed that prayer today, please contact me via DaretoBe@askcoachjamie.com and let me know! I want to celebrate with you! You just made the best decision of your life!! True beauty starts with a relationship with our loving Father!

CONNECT

If you have a relationship with God, take time today to thank Him for His goodness and for choosing you to be a part of His family! When you pray, be sure to pray in faith without doubting. When you end your prayer, say, "I believe it and receive it in Jesus' Name." Then choose to believe it and receive it.

TAKE ACTION

Take time today to soak in how much God loves you. Write down 2 verses that talk about how much God loves you:

_____

_____

_____

_____

_____

_____

_____

_____

_____

_____

_____

_____

_____

_____

PRAY THE WORD

Thank You, Lord, that John 17:3, that I desire to know you above everything else.

Day 8: Loved Beyond Measure

As the Father loved Me, I also have loved you; abide in my love.
John 15:9

WORD STUDY
ABIDE: Greek Word: menō

Continually dwell, Remain as a habit

DEVOTIONAL

I'm going to tell you something that might blow your mind. Did you know that God loves you as much as He loves Jesus? He doesn't love Jesus more than He loves you, but as much as He loves Jesus!

There is nothing that you can do that will get God to love you any more than He does right now. And…there is nothing that you can do to get God to love you any less. God loves you… PERIOD.

God loves you so much! I don't think any of us could ever really hear that enough. So many times we hear well-hearted people saying, "You better watch out, because God's gonna get ya!" Know that God isn't trying to catch you doing something bad. His heart beats for you! He SO loves you that He sent His Son Jesus into the world just for you!

One of the biggest misconceptions in Christian circles is that God allows bad things to happen to you to teach you a lesson. Please hear me in this! Our God does not allow bad things to happen to us! Our God is a good God and to allow bad things to happen would mean that He was mean somewhere in there.

That thought process causes many people to turn away from God, because they think they can do better without Him.

29

John 10:10 tells us that the devil is the one who comes to steal, to kill and to destroy, but Jesus has come to give us life and life more abundantly. If it kills, steals or destroys, it's from Satan. If it gives life, it's from God.

So, why do bad things happen to good people? There is a very real devil that wants to pull us off of the promises of God. He wants to see us lose. Our world is cursed. When Adam sinned in the Garden of Eden, he handed the keys of this world's system over to the devil. As a result, our earth has become cursed and wants to be free. That's why we see tornadoes and hurricanes and earthquakes. And the last reason that bad things happen is because of stupid people. People make bad choices all the time that cause hurt and pain to those around them. None of those things are God. God is good all the time! He doesn't change! Hebrews 13:8 tells us that He is the same yesterday, today and forever!

God is love. Really soak in that truth.

CONNECT
Take time to thank God for how much He loves you. Thank Him for sending His Son to earth to show you how much He loves you. When you pray, be sure to pray in faith without doubting. When you end your prayer, say, "I believe it and receive it in Jesus' Name." Then choose to believe it and receive it.

TAKE ACTION
Is there an area of your life or did something happen in your life that you are struggling to understand? God is there for you and His heart hurts with you. He doesn't like it when He children hurt. Take extra time to talk to God and ask Him to show you His love in this.

_____

_____

_____

_____

_____

_____

_____

_____

_____

_____

_____

_____

_____

_____

_____

_____

_____

_____

_____

_____

_____

_____

_____

PRAY THE WORD

Thank You, Lord, that John 17:23, that You love me as much
You love Jesus.

Day 9: Walk in Truth

My little children, let us not love in word or in tongue,
but in deed and in truth.
1 John 3:18

DEVOTIONAL

Our relationship with God is the most important relationship we will ever have in our life. Take a couple seconds and think about the relationship you have with your best friend. In order to keep that friendship, you need to spend time with them, right? We get to know our friend. We ask them questions and talk to them. We have fun with them. Did you know that this is what a relationship with Jesus looks like as well?

When I think of someone who had a strong relationship with God, I think of Abraham. Abraham was someone who, even though he messed up, sought God with all that he was.

How do we build a strong relationship with the Lord like that? Let's look at the life of Abraham. He had such a strong relationship with the Lord that his faith was counted to him as righteousness, because he believed on the future Jesus who would come and save the world.

Abraham listened to God and obeyed him even when it was inconvenient. In Genesis 12:1 says, "Now the Lord had said to Abram: "Get out of your country, from your family and you're your father's house, to a land that I will show you." I don't know about you, but that had to be challenging. When God called him to leave, he didn't just leave his country, he left is family and everything that meant the most to him. He had no idea where God was taking him next, all he knew was it was an unknown place where he knew no one. But, still, he chose to follow God.

When Abraham moved to his new land with his nephew Lot,

he gave Lot a choice of which land he would like. Lot chose to pitch his tent next to Sodom. From the outside, Sodom probably looked like a place where you could meet a lot of people and have a lot of fun…not the good kind of fun, but the kind of fun that is going to have consequences after a while. Genesis 13:13 says it like this, "But the men of Sodom were exceedingly wicked and sinful against the Lord." Sometimes relationships, especially a relationship with God, will take courage. While Abraham's nephew was enjoying the Sodom lifestyle, Abraham chose his relationship with God to be more important.

A relationship with God also requires trust. Knowing that God has our back and that when He says something to us through His Word, we can believe it.

When God promised Abraham and Sarah, who was barren, that He was going to give them a child and that Abraham was going to be the Father of many nations, it took 25 years for them to see that promise. Circumstances weren't looking that great either. Abraham was 100 years old (way past childbearing years) and Sarah was in her 90s. Physically there was no way for them to have children, yet they chose to believe God and take Him at His word and Isaac was born.

During the teen years, this is the prime time to grow in your relationship with God. After graduating high school, life gets busier. That thought, "one day when I'm older I will spend more time with God" gets shoved to the back burner and forgotten about. If you take time to build our foundation strong now, then eventually you will be like the wise man who built his house on the rock. The storms will come and try to shake you, people will try to get you to move off of the word of God, but you will stand strong.

CONNECT
Have you decided to go all in with your relationship with God? Take time to talk to Him about it today? Maybe you are

all in, talk to Him about how excited you are for your future with Him. If you haven't decided to go all in, talk to God about what's holding you back. When you pray, be sure to pray in faith without doubting. When you end your prayer, say, "I believe it and receive it in Jesus' Name." Then choose to believe it and receive it.

TAKE ACTION

What is something that you can do today to grow stronger in your walk with God? Write it down.

_____

_____

_____

_____

_____

_____

_____

_____

_____

_____

_____

_____

_____

_____

PRAY THE WORD

Thank You, Lord, that 1 John 3:18, You help me to not just say I love others, but that I show Your love by what I do and what I say.

Day 10: Free to Be Me

Therefore, if the Son makes you free,
you shall be free indeed.
John 8:36

WORD STUDY
MAKE: Greek Work: eleutheroō
Deliver, Make free

Make vs Set

Some translations of the Bible read, "If the Son sets you free, you shall be free indeed." However, the original Greek word for this is "make." Why does this matter?

The word "set" implies that someone has the keys to your prison cell and has let you out. The word "make" implies that the person with the keys has now given them to you and now anytime you need to be free, you get to let yourself out.

DEVOTIONAL

I am a natural born thinker. God has definitely given me a gift to think about everything. However, if I'm not careful, I can tend to overthink things, especially if I mess up on something or if I think that something I said didn't come off right. Even if what I did or said wasn't a bad thing, sometimes I will beat myself up mentally and think, "Why did I just do that?" And instead of just leaving it there and moving on, I will go on and on about it in my mind.

Have you ever done that? Have you ever beat yourself up mentally over something that you did or said and it was hard to let it go? A lot of times, I think it's easier for us to forgive someone else for saying or doing something wrong than it is for us to forgive ourselves for saying or doing something wrong.

When we continually beat ourselves up over something we did or said, we are stepping into condemnation. The problem with that is, condemnation is not from God; it's from the devil. Romans 8:1 says, "There is therefore now no condemnation to those who are in Christ Jesus, who do not walk according to the flesh, but according to the Spirit." As Christians, God doesn't want us to walk in condemnation. He wants us free!

Condemnation is what the enemy does to attack our identity...who we are at our core. It says, "You aren't good enough, because..." or "If you really are a child of God, why would you act that way or do this thing?" Condemnation attacks us personally. It finds our faults and attacks every single one of them all at once. It's overwhelming and can lead us to believe that we are not good enough, that we aren't who God says we are.

Conviction is how God deals with us. It focuses on an action and is always specific. It's God saying, "You are my beloved daughter. I want my daughter to live the best life ever, but what you are doing is hurting you." When God convicts us about something we did, He will only point out one thing at a time, not a whole bunch of things at once. He doesn't want His children overwhelmed, but He wants us to win in life. When God does talk to you about something you are doing or not doing, don't beat yourself up over it, just say, "Lord, I'm sorry." Then turn and make the next best decision.

Is there something that God is talking to you about today...or is there something in your past that you are regretting...or has someone done something to you and you feel guilty about it? Talk to God about this. Don't keep holding it inside of you. Ask for forgiveness if you need to. Ask God to help heal you where you are broken if you need to. Then choose to let it go. Don't let what you did define your life. Don't let what was done to you define your life. Let God's love and what Jesus did for you define your life. God wants you free!

CONNECT
Is there something that God is talking to you about today that you need to change or do? It doesn't have to be that you were doing something wrong, it could be that He just desires you to talk to someone about His love. Is there something that has you feeling guilty? Talk to God about it today. When you pray, pray in faith without doubting. When you end your prayer, say, "I believe it and receive it in Jesus' Name." Then choose to believe it and receive it.

TAKE ACTION
Be aware of your thoughts today. Is there anything that you are beating yourself up over mentally? If so, choose to let that go. Ask forgiveness if you need to, but make the choice to let it go. If those thoughts try to keep coming back, tell them to leave because you are made free.

_____

_____

_____

_____

_____

_____

_____

_____

_____

_____

_____

PRAY THE WORD
Thank You, Lord, that John 8:36, for making me free!

Day 11: Living a Thankful Life

Oh, give thanks to the Lord, for He is good. For His mercy endures forever.
Psalm 136:1

WORD STUDY
MERCY: Greek Word: chêsêd

Loving-kindness, Unfailing Love, Beauty, Favor,
Goodness, Compassion

DEVOTIONAL

I recently heard a quote from my pastor, Jim Frease, that made me really think. He said, "It's not happy people who are thankful, but thankful people who are happy." Did you know that living a thankful life will actually cause us to enjoy life better?

When I think of someone who was thankful, I think of the story of the ten lepers that Jesus healed in Luke 17:11-19. Before we get into the story, let's talk a little bit about how lepers used to live in the Bible times.

Lepers in the Old Testament were what priests would call, "unclean." If someone was considered unclean, they were not allowed to have any contact with another human. They had to move out of their own homes and cut off all relationships until a priest considered them clean again. Anyone who was unclean had to wear a certain cloth over themselves so that everyone knew that they were unclean. It didn't just stop there either, if they were ever out in public, they would have to yell out to all of the people around them that they were unclean.

Could you imagine the poor self-image these people would have about themselves? Could you imagine the hurt and the pain they must have felt? Could you imagine the lack of love that people who were considered unclean must have had? A mother who was unclean couldn't spend time with her kids. A husband who was unclean couldn't spend time with his wife. Think about how lonely that had to have been. I couldn't even imagine.

Now, let's go back to Luke 17 where Jesus is entering the village where the ten lepers were. Starting in verses 13 and 14, "And they (the lepers) lifted up their voices and said, 'Jesus, Master, have mercy on us!' So, when Jesus saw them, He said to them, 'Go, show yourselves to the priests.' And so it was that as they went, they were cleansed."

This is when something changes for one of the ten lepers. We know that Jesus had just healed all ten of these lepers, correct? But something happened right after their healing took place. Luke 17:15-16 says, "And one of them, when he saw that he was healed, returned, and with a loud voice glorified God, and fell down on his face and at His feet, giving Him thanks."

Let's think about this for a minute. How many of the lepers were healed? Ten, right? How many turned around, went back to Jesus and thanked Him? Only one. If you go on to read verses 17 through 19, you will see that even though all ten lepers were healed, only the one that turned to give God thanks was made whole.

What's the difference between being healed and being made whole? With the nine men who were healed, the symptoms of the leprosy were now gone. However, the scars and disfigurements that come as a result of the leprosy were still there. For the one leper who was made whole, he was not just healed of the symptoms, but all of the scars and disfigurements as well. It looked as if he never even had leprosy to begin with. Pretty amazing right? No scars, no disfigurements!

The one leper who turned around, went back to Jesus and

thanked God for his healing, shows us that the more thankful we are, the more whole we become. "It's not happy people who are thankful, but thankful people who are happy!"

If you're struggling in any area or if there is something on the inside of you that feels broken or not good enough, know that God can heal that hurt and make you as if you never had those pains in the first place. He can completely wipe away the scars that you have been holding onto on the inside. He has all the healing you need if you just receive it. When you find yourself getting down about something, turn those thoughts around and begin to thank God...not for whatever is pulling you down, but because He is good and is healing you of those things. When you stand on God's Word and you continue to thank Him for His goodness, you will find yourself over time receiving the healing you need.

CONNECT
Is there an area of your life that has felt broken? Or do you struggle sometimes with not feeling good enough or measuring up to those around you? Take time to talk to God today. He wants you to receive His love. When you pray, pray in faith without doubting. When you end your prayer, say, "I believe it and receive it in Jesus' Name." Then choose to believe it and receive it.

TAKE ACTION
Write down 5 things that you can thank God for today:

1. _____

_____

_____

_____

_____

2. _____
   _____
   _____
   _____
   _____

3. _____
   _____
   _____
   _____
   _____

4. _____
   _____
   _____
   _____
   _____

5. _____
   _____
   _____
   _____
   _____

PRAY THE WORD

Thank You, Lord, for you are good. Your mercy endures forever.

Day 12: You are Valuable

For we are His workmanship, created in Christ Jesus
for good works, which God prepared beforehand
that we should walk in them.
Ephesians 2:10

WORD STUDY
WORKMANSHIP: Greek Word: poiēma

God is the Master Designer and you are His
Masterpiece.

DEVOTIONAL

Have you ever thought about what makes a masterpiece a masterpiece? I mean, why is Van Gogh's "The Starry Night" such an incredible piece of art? Someone seeing it for the first time might say that it's just a bunch of swirling colors that make up a picture. However, others say it's one of the most incredible pieces of art that has ever been created. Why is that?

What makes a masterpiece so valuable? Did you know that there actually is a specific formula to determining the value of a masterpiece? Here are four ways that experts decide how valuable a masterpiece really is:

1. By how rare it is-is there anything else like it?
2. By if it's an original-is it an original piece or is it a copy?
3. By the author who created it-are they highly sought after?
4. By the price that someone is willing to pay for it.

So, what does this have to do with us? We are a masterpiece! God's very own special creation.

1. You are rare! There is no one else in this world like you. You are one-of-a-kind! Did you know that all humans share

2. 99% of the same DNA in their bodies? It's in that 1% that makes us so different and so unique. You are rare!

3. You are an original! Before the world even began, God thought about every single characteristic about you down to the number of hairs that are on your head. He tells us in Jeremiah 1:5, that He knew you before you were in your mom's womb. He knew and approved of you before the world even began! He created you and He was pleased with His creation.

4.The Artist that created you is the greatest creator ever! He couldn't wait to form you in your mother's womb and develop a relationship with you!

5.You were bought with the ultimate price anyone could ever pay! You were bought with the blood of Jesus! You are priceless! Hebrews 12:1-2 says, "Looking unto Jesus, the author and finisher of *our* faith, who for the joy that was set before Him endured the cross, despising the shame, and has sat down at the right hand of the throne of God. Do you know who that joy was that was set before Him? That joy that got Him to look passed the pain and torture of the cross was us. Jesus paid the ultimate price so that we could live forever in a relationship with Him.

CONNECT
Has the thought of you being a masterpiece sunk in, yet? It can be tough to grasp how incredible God has made us? Take time to talk to Him today and ask Him reveal to you how much He loves you and why it is He made you the way he did. When you end your prayer, say, "I believe it and receive it in Jesus' Name." Then choose to believe it and receive it.

TAKE ACTION
Write out Ephesians 2:10. Take some time to let it sink in and then right down what God is saying about you.

_____

_____

_____

_____

_____

_____

_____

_____

_____

_____

_____

_____

_____

_____

_____

_____

_____

_____

_____

_____

PRAY THE WORD

Thank You, Lord that Ephesians 2:10, that I am Your master-piece. I have been created in Christ for good works, which You prepared for me before the world began and that I get to walk out that plan.

Day 13: Identity Leads to Security

Let us therefore come boldly to the throne of grace, that we may obtain mercy and find grace to help in time of need.
Hebrews 4:16

DEVOTIONAL

We all have the need to feel a sense of security. None of us like feeling insecure. When we are secure in who we are, we are able to trust the people God has surrounded us with. We're able to be who God created us to be instead of trying to be someone we're not. However, being secure in who we are is easier said than done in most cases.

I remember when I was a teen, one of the things that drove me the craziest was when my friends were themselves around me, but would act like someone else when they were around other people. My friends would try so hard to get those people to like them. It drove me crazy.

For example, a friend of mine couldn't stand rap music. Her brother would listen to it and she would get so annoyed. However, this same friend had a guy that she really liked start talking to her. He was talking to her about how much he liked this particular rap band. Her response wasn't, "I'm not a fan." Instead she would say, "Me too!" I couldn't understand why she would lie just to get someone to like her.

But really, I was dealing with the same thing my friends were: insecurity. My insecurity didn't come in the form of pretending to be someone I wasn't, mine was different. I would walk into a room, hear people laughing and automatically think they were laughing at me. They had no clue that I was even going to be walking in the room. I would end up sitting off to the side of the room by myself wishing I could be someone else. See, my friends liked the idea of trying to be someone they weren't in order to get people to like them. I liked to wish I was someone I wasn't so I could get people to like me. Insecurity is not a fun place to live.

If you are struggling with liking who you are, know that God created you just the way you are and you are beautiful! The more confident you become, the more people will be drawn to you. You don't need to change who you are to gain friends.

Choose to take in what God says about you above what anyone else says about you. The more you get a revelation of how much God loves you and how incredibly He created you to be, the more confident and secure you will become.

CONNECT
Is there an area of your life that you don't feel confident in? Maybe it's the way you look or maybe you struggle to make friends. Ask God to reveal to you how much He loves you and when you pray, be sure to pray in faith without doubting. When you end your prayer, say, "I believe it and receive it in Jesus' Name." Then choose to believe it and receive it.

TAKE ACTION
Talk to God today about something that's been weighing on your heart. Write down how you can overcome that insecurity or challenge. If you can't think of any to write, write down something that you have applied from these past couple days that has really made a change in your life.

_____

_____

_____

_____

_____

_____

_____

_____

_____

_____

_____

_____

_____

_____

_____

_____

_____

_____

_____

_____

_____

_____

_____

_____

_____

_____

_____

PRAY THE WORD

Thank You, Lord, that Hebrews 4:16, I can come boldly to Your throne of grace. Thank You, that I get to obtain mercy and find grace to help me in my time of need.

Day 14: Guard Your Identity

Keep your heart with all diligence for out of it
spring the issues of life._
Proverbs 4:23

WORD STUDY
KEEP YOUR HEART

Protecting your mind, your will (your choices), and your emotions by watching what you see, hear and speak.

DILIGENCE: Hebrew Word: mishmâr

Doing little things for a long time until it makes a big difference.

DEVOTIONAL

Once we start to get a revelation of who it is that God says we are, the enemy will try to attack us to steal away that truth. This is why it's so important that we guard our identity so that the enemy or other people can't take it from us.

How do we guard our identity though? Guarding our identity starts with making sure that we are getting into the Word of God every day and choosing to believe what His Word says. It also begins with protecting our thoughts.

"Is it really even possible to protect our thoughts?" It is possible. We protect our thoughts by protecting what we choose to look at. If something inappropriate pops up on your computer or on your phone are you turning your head away from it and getting rid of it as fast as you can?

We also protect our thoughts by being cautious about what we are listening to. Do the shows that we're watching have good morals? Is the music that we're listening to glorifying

God? Are the friends we are surrounding ourselves with encouraging us and building us and others up?

And the last way we protect our thoughts is by being cautious of the words that are coming out of our mouths. Are we saying things that we want to see happen in our lives? Our words are like a thermostat that we use to heat or cool our homes. If we set the temperature on that thermostat to 70 degrees, eventually we will see 70 degrees in our home. The same thing is true with our words. Whatever we speak over ourselves or those around us we will eventually see come true in our lives and their lives.

2 Corinthians 10:4-5 tells us, "Our weapons of warfare are mighty in God for pulling down strongholds, casting down arguments and every high thing that exalts itself against the knowledge of God, bringing every thought into captivity to the obedience of Christ."

The biggest battle we will fight as Christians is the battle of our minds (our thoughts). In 2 Corinthians 10:4-5, we see the word stronghold. A stronghold is basically a thought process. Think of a stronghold like a water slide. You go to the top and it shoots you out at the same place at the bottom every single time. Our thoughts are like that. If we think the same thought for an extended period of time, we start to believe that it's true. Once we start to believe that it's true, it becomes a stronghold in our minds. After it becomes a stronghold, we begin acting like it's the truth and will see it happen in our lives.

When these thoughts are negative, they act as a fortress that surrounds our thought processes. They keep us locked tight and that can be hard to break free from.

Since strongholds start in the mind, it's important to do like 2 Corinthians 10:4-5 says, to take every thought captive. What that means is, if you catch yourself thinking a thought you know God wouldn't agree with, turn it around to something

He would agree with. We do this by changing what we continually see, what we continually hear and what we continually say.

For example, let's say the thought, "I'm not good at anything. Why am I even here?" pops into your head. We have a choice; we can choose to believe that thought and start thinking about all the ways we aren't good enough or we can choose to not believe it and change the thought. Since God's Word says in Jeremiah 29:11 that God has a plan for your life, you can change that thought to, "No! God says that I was created with a purpose and I am going to find out what that purpose is for my life!"

CONNECT
Is there a stronghold in your life, a lie that you have been believing, that you know is the opposite of what God says about you? Take time to talk to God about it today. When you pray, pray in faith without doubting. When you end your prayer, say, "I believe it and receive it in Jesus' Name." Then choose to believe it and receive it.

TAKE ACTION
Take time today to think about what strongholds are holding you back. What are some verses that you can start speaking today to conquer those strongholds? Write them out below.

_____

_____

_____

_____

_____

_____

_____

_____

_____

_____

_____

_____

_____

_____

_____

_____

_____

_____

_____

_____

_____

_____

_____

_____

_____

_____

PRAY THE WORD

Thank You, Lord, that Proverbs 4:23, I will keep my heart pure by watching what I put in my eyes, speak out of my mouth and listen with my ears.

Part 2:
Dare to Be…
Confident

Day 1: Created with a Purpose

Before I formed you in the womb I knew you;
before you were born I sanctified you;
I ordained you a prophet to the nations.
Jeremiah 1:5

<u>WORD STUDY</u>
SANCTIFIED: Hebrew Word: qâdash
Set apart

ORDAINED: Hebrew Word: nâthan
Appointed

PROPHET: Hebrew Word: nâbîy'
One who is called, appointed

DEVOTIONAL

Growing up, I was an average girl, just getting through life one day at a time. I got good grades, not because I was super smart, but because I studied really hard. I was okay at playing sports. I was okay at drawing. I was okay at singing and playing instruments, but I wasn't really great at anything.

I will tell you something I was really good at, though. I was really good at looking at everyone else and wishing I could be like them: I wished I was prettier; I wished I was smarter; I wished I was sportier; I wished I could sing and play my instrument better.

Do you ever feel this way? Did you know that God created you unique and that you have your own set of unique gifts and talents? Maybe you can't see those gifts and talents right now, like I couldn't, but they're there. God created you so special, so unique and He wants to use you to make a difference in this world!

You were created with a purpose! Your purpose looks

nothing like anyone else's purpose, because it is unique to you and your God-given gifts and talents.

I love the promise from God in Jeremiah 1:5. God is telling Jeremiah that before he was even in his mother's womb, God knew him. That word "knew" means that God thought up everything about him. He created him with such unique gifts and talents and created him with a specific purpose. This promise isn't just for Jeremiah. God's saying the same thing about you. Before He formed YOU in the womb, He knew you. Before YOU were born, He set you apart and called you for a specific purpose.

As a teen, I know that it can be challenging when you aren't sure what you're good at or maybe you have no clue what it is that you are supposed to do for the rest of your life. It can also be a challenge if you do know what your unique gifts and talents are and are trying to make them look like everyone else's that share similar gifts and talents. God created you uniquely.

But for each one of us, God does give us a clue to what our purpose looks like. In Exodus 9:16, He tells us, "But indeed for this purpose I have raised you up, that I may show My power in you, and that My name may be declared in all the earth."

The purpose that God has for our life will always lead us to make an impact for His kingdom. There are so many broken and hurting people out there, just look around. God wants to use us to touch and bless their lives. Our purpose is so much greater than we even realize. When we walk in our purpose, though, it will bring us so much joy and such an incredible life.

But what if we aren't really sure what it is that we're supposed to do? Or what if we know what our gifts and talents are, but we're not sure how God wants us to use them? Take some time and think about the answers to these questions:

1. What motivates you to keep going when life gets tough?

2. What energizes you? (And I don't mean sugar or coffee)

3. What touches your heart in a good way?

4. What makes you righteously angry? Righteous anger is something that hurts your heart and you want to see it changed.

CONNECT

Take time to talk to God about what it is that He wants you to do and how He wants you to use your gifts and talents for Him. Thank Him for showing you what it is that He wants you to see. When you pray, pray in faith without doubting. When you end your prayer, say, "I believe it and receive it in Jesus' Name." Then choose to believe it and receive it.

TAKE ACTION

Answer the four questions from above:

1. What motivates you to keep going when things get tough?

_____

_____

_____

_____

_____

_____

_____

2. What energizes you?

_____

_____

_____

_____

_____

_____

_____

3. What touches your heart and moves you to tears in a good way?

_____

_____

_____

_____

_____

4. What makes you righteously angry? Righteous anger is something that hurts your heart and you want to change it.

_____

_____

_____

_____

_____

PRAY THE WORD

Thank You, Lord, Jeremiah 1:5, that before You formed me in the womb You knew me; before I was born You set me apart and called me for a specific purpose.

Day 2: Purpose is Found in the Lord

Many plans are in a man's mind,
but it is the Lord's purpose for him that will stand.
Proverbs 19:21 AMPC

DEVOTIONAL

Have you ever stopped yourself from doing something that you really wanted to do or knew you should do, because you were afraid what someone else might think of you? I know I have so many times. I used to second guess myself about everything I did and honestly, I was terrified to try anything new. I eventually got to the point that I would only try something new if my friends were going to do it.

If we aren't careful, we begin to find our value and purpose in what our friends or other people might think about us instead of finding our value and purpose in what God thinks about us. The truth is, we will never find peace, joy or even purpose if we are always living by the approval of others.

For the majority of us, we desire to be popular. We want to be fashionable. We want to be liked by everyone and we never want to be alone. We want to be accepted...and that is perfectly normal. However, the problem with trying to get approval from people is that...people change. One day they like you, the next day they don't...and it has nothing to do with you! We all have emotions. One minute our emotions are up and the next minute they're down. It all depends on the circumstances and what's going on around us.

When we choose to get our approval from God, the great news is, He never changes. He loves us and accepts us and wants to be with us every single day of our lives!

Maybe you are like I was as a teen. I was shy and very much an introvert...I would rather watch people than be the center of attention. I had a very small group of friends and if those friends weren't around, I had nobody. It felt like such a lonely place for me. Or maybe you're like my son: outgoing and very much an extrovert...you like being the center of attention. That can be a lonely place, too, especially when everyone is gone and it's just you.

No matter what your personality is, know that God created you on purpose. Whether or not you know what your God-given purpose is, you can live with purpose every single day. There is someone that God wants you to reach out to today; there is someone He wants you to smile at and say hi to today; there is someone He wants you to bless today.

Everyday, God puts people in our path so that we can make their day just a little brighter. When we live with purpose each day, God is able to reveal to us His ultimate purpose for our life. All you have to do is be available for God to use you. God isn't looking at whether or not we are capable of doing something specific, He just wants to know that we are available for Him to use us.

CONNECT
When you go places, do you leave yourself extra time to think about how to bless others? Or are you always in a rush? Take time today to talk to God about who He wants you to bless today. When you pray, pray in faith without doubting. When you end your prayer, say, "I believe it and receive it in Jesus' Name." Then choose to believe it and receive it.

TAKE ACTION
What is one thing you can do today to reach out and encourage or bless someone? What is God speaking to your heart?

_____

_____

_____

_____

_____

_____

_____

_____

_____

_____

_____

_____

_____

_____

_____

_____

_____

_____

_____

_____

_____

_____

_____

PRAY THE WORD

Thank You, Lord, Proverbs 19:21, that Your purpose is the one that will stand in my life.

Day 3: What's Holding You Back?

There is therefore now no condemnation to those who are in Christ Jesus, who do not walk according to the flesh, but according to the Spirit. For the law of the Spirit of life in Christ Jesus has made me free from the law of sin and death.
Romans 8:1-2

DEVOTIONAL

If we compromise who we are to get someone to like us, eventually we will lose who we really are.

Usually, we don't set out to compromise who we are, we don't go out and say, "Oh yeah, I want to get stuck in this really bad sin;" or "I want to make this really poor choice that will have major consequences for me later in life." Compromise always starts out by making small decisions that we don't think really matter. Maybe we start out with a really small lie so that we can make ourselves look better in front of our friends...or maybe we start out with saying something we know we shouldn't so that we don't look bad... or posting a picture that we know we shouldn't be posting.

However, those small choices will one day lead to big consequences. Compromise is a slippery slope. The more we compromise, the harder it is to stop, and the more slippery it gets until we wake up one day and we don't even recognize who we are.

King David, you know the same David that fought Goliath? He went down the slippery slope of compromise. His started with a small, little peek at Bathsheba while she was bathing. He could have chosen to look away and ask God for forgiveness, but instead, he let this choice lead to adultery, then to lying, then to murder, then to guilt and no longer recognizing who he was anymore.

Is there a choice you've made, even if it's small, to compromise to get people to like you or to make yourself look better? You may have even walked away from the situation saying, "Why did I say that?" or "Why did I do that?" At that moment, you have a choice, to continue down that road or to go to God and ask Him to forgive you.

Choose to make a decision today not to compromise who you are or what you believe…make a firm choice not to go down that road. However, if you do make a choice to compromise, go right away to God and talk to Him about it. Now is the time to build the foundation of who you are and what you believe. Make that foundation so strong that you don't compromise no matter what.

Maybe there is something you compromised on in your past that you haven't been able to forgive yourself for…or maybe there is something that you're struggling with today that you feel guilty about and you are believing lies about yourself that you aren't good enough.

Proverbs 28:13 tells us that he who covers his sins will not prosper, but whoever confesses and forsakes them will have mercy. This is basically saying that that if we continue to hide that choice we made like nothing has happened, hide the guilt that we are feeling, or hide the lies that we are choosing to believe, there is no way to win. We can't win in life when we are tearing ourselves down and beating ourselves up.

But there is good news. The end of the verse says, "but whoever confesses and forsakes them will have mercy." Talk to God about what's going on and if you need to, talk to someone you can trust…preferably an adult who loves the Lord and loves you. Maybe there is a youth pastor, a youth leader or your parents that you can go to. They want to help you to overcome this, because they want you to win in life.
I John 1:9 says that if we confess our sins, God is faithful and just to forgive us our sins and cleanse us from all unrighteousness. That phrase, "cleanse us from all

unrighteousness" means any guilt that is associated with that sin: guilt that is holding us back.

That sin or that guilt that is trying to hold you back has not defeated you. Don't give up! The power of God that raised Jesus from the dead lives in you and it is greater than the power of any sin...no matter how recent or how long ago it happened. You don't have to hold onto that guilt anymore!

CONNECT
Take time today to ask God to help you stand strong in your beliefs and in who He created you to be. When you end your prayer, say, "I believe it and receive it in Jesus' Name." Then choose to believe it and receive it.

TAKE ACTION
Make a decision today to stand strong in your beliefs and in who God created you to be. Make a choice not to compromise. If you have friends that you see who are compromising, pull them aside and talk to them in love. Let them know that you care about them and want to see them win.

_____

_____

_____

_____

_____

_____

PRAY THE WORD
Thank You, Lord, that I John 1:9, if I mess up and go to you confessing what I have done, that you are faithful to forgive me. I thank You for not only forgiving me, but for taking away the guilt that is associated with the choice I made.

Day 4: It Starts with God

But seek first the kingdom of God and His righteousness,
and all these things shall be added to you.
Matthew 6:33

WORD STUDY
FIRST: Greek Word: prōton

At the beginning; first of all

When we put God first in our life, He won't just provide for us, but He will bless us beyond what we can imagine!

DEVOTIONAL

Whatever we put first in our life, will determine the attitudes and the decisions we will make.

I love how God started out the Bible. The very first four words in Genesis 1:1 say, "In the beginning, God..." I don't think this was done by accident; I think it was intentional. God knows that when we put Him first in any area of our life, those are the areas that will be the most blessed.

For so long, I had the habit of turning off my alarm on my phone (who actually uses an alarm clock anymore...right?) and as soon as I turned off the alarm, I would open my phone and go straight to social media to see what happened while I was sleeping (because a lot happens in eight hours, right?).

The problem was, I never knew what I was going to see on social media. Maybe I would see a post that was encouraging and inspiring. Unfortunately, I didn't see those posts very often. Most of the time, I would see a post that was negative or one that hurt my heart, because it was so sad. I didn't realize how these posts that I was seeing were setting the tone for my day. Sometimes it would be positive and sometimes it would be negative...no wonder I had a challenge with being overwhelmed, stressed out and anxious all the time.

Because I chose to go to my phone and the world before I went to God, I would always start my day by barely keeping my head above the water. It wasn't until I decided that I was going to start putting God first above social media that I actually started my day on stronger ground...or as they say, "walking on the water with Jesus."

One thing I love about God is that He never changes. I know when I go to God, I'm going to be encouraged and inspired. Hebrews 13:8 tells us that God is the same yesterday, today and forever. God is good all the time. He doesn't change, He's always good and He knows exactly what we need.

Philippians 4:19 says that He provides all our needs according to His riches in glory by Christ Jesus. When we put God first, all of our needs are met. Jeremiah 29:11 says that He only has good plans for our life...plans that give us a hope and a future. When we start our day out with God, we get to start the day walking on water, not drowning by all of the problems of the world.

That sounds great, but practically, what does it look like to put God first in our day? I know with early mornings, the last thing we want to do is start getting up even earlier than we have to. However, it is so important! I'm not asking you to set your alarm for an hour earlier. I'm not even asking you to set your alarm for 30 minutes early. What I want to encourage you to do, though, is to set your alarm for just 15 minutes before you normally do.

Turn on one praise and worship song and spend some focused time on praising the Lord. Then, afterwards, take five minutes connect with God through prayer. Ask Him to help you be a light to those around you and thank Him for good things that He is doing in your life right now. Then ask

Him to help you understand what He wants you to see in the Bible. Then, grab your Bible and connect with God for five minutes while reading the Word. If you need a place to start with reading, I encourage you to start either in the book of John or in Psalm 91. The book of John was written by a disciple who really understood how much God loved Him. Psalm 91 is a great chapter to read to understand God's protection over you.

CONNECT

Have you made it a habit to spend time with God, when you first get up? If not, talk to God about helping you to establish that habit. If you have, talk to God about helping you to receive His love for you even more today. When you pray, pray in faith without doubting. When you end your prayer, say, "I believe it and receive it in Jesus' Name." Then choose to believe it and receive it.

TAKE ACTION

What is one area of your life that you can focus on when it comes to connecting with God in the mornings?

Praise: Are you thinking about the words that you're singing to the Lord?

_____

_____

_____

_____

_____

_____

_____

Prayer: Are you connecting with God or watching the clock?

_____

_____

_____

_____

_____

_____

_____

Bible: Are you slowing down when you read the Bible to make sure you're getting something out of it or reading it just to get it done?

_____

_____

_____

_____

_____

_____

_____

PRAY THE WORD

Thank You, Lord, that Matthew 6:33, when I seek Your kingdom first and your righteousness, You provide all my needs and you bless me above and beyond.

Day 5: The Power of Praise

Sing to the Lord, for He has done excellent things;
this is known in all the earth.
Isaiah 12:5

DEVOTIONAL

Have you ever stood through praise and worship at your church and sang the songs, but never really thought about the words you were singing? I remember being 19 years old and the thought hit me…"these words that I'm singing, they actually mean something." It was during that moment that I took a step back in my mind and started really listening to the words that I was singing. I couldn't believe how powerful these words were.

The word, "worship" in the Greek means: to adore, to fall forward on your knees and kiss the face of God as an act of love for a Father who loves us so much. Worship is an intimate time of praise between us and God. It literally means, "to kiss the face of God." So, every time we are worshipping God, we are kissing the face of God and saying, "I love you, Daddy!"

I heard a teaching from one of my mentors, Pastor Rick Renner, and it painted a picture so beautifully of what the word "worship" really means.

This is what he shared: Psalm 22:3 in the King James Version of the Bible tells us that God inhabits the praises of his people. The word "inhabit" means that God feels so honored and blessed by our praises that when He hears us, He comes and sits down with us. When God comes to sit down with us, He brings His glory with Him. When God brings His glory, He brings everything good with it that we could every possibly need in our life.

If you are having a challenge and need to be delivered from

something, God has already provided the way out. If you are fighting off sickness or pain, God has already provided healing. If you are struggling with anxiety and aren't sure what to do about it, the answers are there! Everything we need is there and we receive it when we praise.

Acts 16 paints a beautiful picture of worship in action. Verse 25 says, "But at midnight Paul and Silas were praying and singing hymns to God, and the prisoners were listening to them." During this time, Paul and Silas were in prison. In this prison cell, prisoners were not all kept together in the same place so when this passage talks about the prisoners listening to them, it shows us that Paul and Silas were praying and praising with everything they had within them.

Acts 16:26 then goes on to say, "Suddenly there was a great earthquake, so that the foundations of the prison were shaken; and immediately all the doors were opened and everyone's chains were loosed."

See Paul and Silas knew that they were in big trouble. If they were to stay in the prison, they would have been put to death. Instead of getting depressed and complaining about their circumstances, they chose to praise God with all that was within them. When we praise, it puts us in a position to receive God's blessing and His goodness.

There are times when the circumstances we are going through are tough. Things aren't going so well. The last thing we want to do in those situations is praise God. However, the best time to praise God is when we don't feel like it. Praise helps us to see things from God's perspective. Praise repels depression and brings joy into our lives. Praise brings healing and releases worry.

Hebrews 13:15 says to let us continually offer the sacrifice of praise to God, that is the fruit of our lips, giving thanks to His name. It's a sacrifice, because it isn't always easy to do.

How do we praise? We can praise God by singing worship music that has lyrics that line up with the Bible. We can make up our own worship songs, singing to the Lord. We can play a musical instrument for the Lord. We can even just take time to thank Him for how good He is.

CONNECT

Take time today to thank God for His goodness. If there is something that you need to be delivered from or an area of your life you could use some wisdom, talk to Him. He loves spending time with you. When you pray, pray in faith without doubting. When you end your prayer, say, "I believe it and receive it in Jesus' Name." Then choose to believe it and receive it.

TAKE ACTION

What are 5 things that you can thank God for today?

1. _____

_____

_____

_____

_____

_____

2. _____

_____

_____

_____

_____

_____

3. _____

_____

_____

_____

_____

_____

4. _____

_____

_____

_____

_____

_____

5. _____

_____

_____

_____

_____

_____

_____

_____

PRAY THE WORD

Thank You, Lord, that Hebrews 13:15, I will continually offer a sacrifice of praise to you, giving thanks to Your Name.

Day 6: Prayer that Get Results

Confess your trespasses to one another, and pray for one another; that you may be healed. The effective fervent prayer of a righteous man avails much (has tremendous power).
_James 5:16

WORD STUDY
EFFECTUAL: Greek Word: energeō

To be effective; energize
God can accomplish great things through our prayers.

DEVOTIONAL

Prayer was probably the one area of my life that I struggled with the most as a young Christian. I didn't know if I was praying the correct way for God to hear me. Honestly, I felt like I was just talking to myself. A lot of times, I think we just pray because it makes us feel better, but many times we don't expect things to work out.

Have you ever heard the phrase, "God, if it's your will..."? For example, "If it's God's will, you will heal them." "If it's God's will, they will come to know the Lord." I think many times we say these phrases, because we honestly don't know what God's will is for that certain situation. Did you know that for many circumstances we can actually find out the will of God? The Bible is God's will. If you're not sure if it's God's will, dig into His Word. If it's a question like "What college should I attend?" Well, that is not going to be found in the Bible directly, but in James 1:5, it says if anyone lacks wisdom, let him ask of God and God will give it to him. The key to asking is to be sure to ask in faith.

Did you know that there is only one type of prayer that God can answer? It's not the prayer of desperation. It's actually

71

the prayer of faith.

Mark 11:22-25 says, "So Jesus answered and said to them, "Have faith in God. For assuredly, I say to you, whoever says to this mountain, 'Be removed and be cast into the sea,' and does not doubt in his heart, but believes that those things he says will be done, he will have whatever he says. Therefore, I say to you, whatever things you ask when you pray, believe that you receive *them,* and you will have *them.*"

In order to really understand how to pray in faith, we need to first understand what faith is. Hebrews 11:1 tells us, "Now faith is the substance of things hoped for, the evidence of things not seen." That word "substance" means, "confidence." And the word "hope" means, "a fervent expectation of good." It basically means that you aren't wishing, but instead you strongly believe and are completely confident that what you are believing for, you will see happen. So, let's read it like this, "Now faith is being confident of the good things that you are expecting to see in your life. The evidence of things not seen."

Now that we know what faith is, how do we grow our faith? Romans 10:17 tells us "faith comes by hearing, and hearing by the word of God." That word "hearing" in the Greek means not just to hear it once, but over and over again until it moves from something we know in our head to something we strongly believe in our heart.

So, when we think of faith this way, it helps us to see prayer differently. When we pray in faith, we find verses on the area we are believing for. We read them and speak them over and over again and choose to believe them; that is when our faith grows. When we pray in faith, that's when we see results.

CONNECT
Is there an area of your life that you've been praying over or that has been on your heart? Find several verses in the Bible

on those areas, stand on those verses and watch your faith grow. Then, take time to talk to God. When you pray, pray in faith without doubting. When ending your prayer, say, "I believe it and receive it in Jesus' Name." Then choose to believe it and receive it.

TAKE ACTION

Grab a blank notebook or a binder with notebook paper. We are creating a Life Book. Think about an area of your life that you could grow stronger in: maybe you worry a lot and could grow in your peace; maybe you have a challenge choosing a good attitude and could grow in your joy; maybe you are fighting off pain or an illness and you need healing; maybe you are believing God for friends who love Him.

At the top of the first page, write the topic you're choosing to focus on. On the lines below, write verses that you're using to build your faith. For an example on healing, you could write, "Psalm 107:20-He (God) sent forth His word and healed them, and delivered them from their destructions."

Next, rewrite that verse as a prayer over your life, "Thank You, Lord, that Psalm 107:20, You sent forth Your Word and healed me. I have been delivered from destruction, in Jesus' Name."

Do this for 2-3 verses, then pray them out load every time you wake up and every time you go to bed. Over time, you will find your faith beginning to grow stronger in that area. t When you do, add a couple more verses or a new topic and do the same with them.

PRAY THE WORD

Thank You, Lord, that James 5:16, You can accomplish great things through my prayers of faith.

Day 7: The Transforming Power of the Word

But Jesus answered and said, "It is written, Man shall not live by bread alone, but by every word that proceeds out of the mouth of God."
Matthew 4:4

DEVOTIONAL

Have you ever heard of the "Read the Bible in One Year" Challenge? You may have even done this or tried this. I have not. I remember the first time I heard that and thought, "That sounds like a great idea!" Then, I looked at the reading plan and was like… "uh…I don't think so!" I knew if I took that challenge, I could probably do it, but I also knew that if I took that challenge, I would probably not understand a single word I was reading. I would be taking the challenge just to say I did it. I wanted to grow in my walk with the Lord.

So many times we read the Bible just because it's something we are supposed to do, but I want to ask you a question and I want you to answer honestly. Have you ever read the Bible just to get it done and not really to connect with God and learn? I know I have.

Reading the Bible isn't about getting a certain amount of verses or chapters every day, it's all about connecting with God. Instead of reading the Bible to check off a list, start thinking about, "What did I just read?" and "How can I apply this to my life today?"

Psalm 119:9-11 in the NIV says, "How can a young person stay on the path of purity? By living according to your word. I seek you with all my heart; do not let me stray from your commands. I have hidden your word in my heart that I might not sin against you."

One way that I like reading the Bible is to read a small

74

section of a chapter at a time. I like reading it this way because the verses build upon one another and it helps with making sure that we aren't taking God's Word out of context. Reading a couple verses and getting something out of it is more important than reading a whole chapter and getting nothing out of it.

Now, you may not have a revelation every time you read the Word and that's okay. You are still getting the Word in you. Just ask God in those moments to help you understand what He wants you to see.

If you're wondering where to start with reading the Bible, here's a great plan that I recommend. Start in the book of John. John had such a revelation of how much God loved him that he actually called himself, "The Disciple that Jesus Loved." When John walked this earth with Jesus, He was only between the ages of 13 and 16 and was able to do incredible things for the Lord, because of that revelation.

When you're done reading the book of John head over to Ephesians. Paul had such an incredible insight on who God says we are and how much He loves us.

CONNECT
How are you doing in your daily time in the Word. Has it been a struggle for you to be consistent? Are you sometimes just checking off the days, just because it's something you're supposed to do? Talk to God and ask Him to help you grow in your desire to spend time in His Word. Ask Him to show you what it is that He wants you to see. When you pray, pray in faith without doubting. When you end your prayer, say, "I believe it and receive it in Jesus' Name." Then choose to believe it and receive it.

TAKE ACTION
If you aren't sure where to start reading in your Bible time with God, I encourage you to begin in the book of John.

Read one small section and ask yourself: what does this mean to me? How can I apply these principles to my life?

_____

_____

_____

_____

_____

_____

_____

_____

_____

_____

_____

_____

_____

_____

_____

_____

_____

_____

PRAY THE WORD

Thank You, Lord, that Psalm 119:9-11, that I am keeping my life pure by living according to Your Word. I am seeking You with my whole heart. I have hidden Your word in my heart so I stay faithful to You.

Day 8: God's Ultimate Plan for You

For this is good and acceptable in the sight of God our Savior, who desires all men to be saved and to come to the knowledge of the Truth.
1 Timothy 2:3-4

DEVOTIONAL

So many times we get caught up on the things we don't know that we totally miss what we do know. I remember growing up thinking, "I have no clue what I'm supposed to do in life. I'm good at several things, but I'm not really great at anything. I felt like since I had no clue what I was going to do in my life, that I must not have a purpose. I felt stuck and truthfully, I didn't feel like that I really mattered when it came to the kingdom of God.

Was I ever wrong about that!! That is the farthest thing from the Truth! God's ultimate plan for our lives, we can actually walk out today...whether or not we know our God-given purpose.

John 17:3 is a part of a beautiful prayer that Jesus is praying about His purpose and why God sent Him. Verse 3 says, "And this is eternal life, that they may know You, the only true God, and Jesus Christ whom You have sent." Who do you think the "they" is in that verse? That's you! That's me! That's all of us. Our purpose in life is to know our incredibly loving Father, the one True God, and Jesus Christ!

However, God's ultimate plan doesn't just stop there. 1 Peter 3:15-16 in The Passion Translation says, "but give reverent honor in your hearts to [God]. And if anyone asks about the hope living within you, always be ready to explain your faith with gentleness and respect."

Every single day at school, out in public, everywhere we go, we see people that are depressed and hurting. They need the hope that we have living on the inside of us.

How do you explain your faith, though? We can immediately begin to think thoughts like, "I don't know the Bible enough to share it with someone else," or, "What do I say?" or "How do I do this?" Know that sharing your faith is the same thing as sharing your story of what God has done in your life.

Maybe you didn't find Jesus until recently and your life was a mess before. Share how God changed you on the inside. Or maybe you're like my husband who grew up a Christian. Share with them how God is transforming you. What has God done for you that has helped you? You have a story, don't feel like it's insignificant. Share it!

CONNECT
Take time today to talk to God about what He wants you to share with those around you. Ask Him to show you who He wants to share your story with. When you pray, pray in faith without doubting. When you end your prayer, say, "I believe it and receive it in Jesus' Name." Then choose to believe it and receive it.

TAKE ACTION
Who is God talking to you about when it comes to sharing your story? When sharing your story, focus on sharing from your heart, not saying everything perfectly. Be honest and be real. Keep it simple. Here's a guideline to help you think:

What was your life like before you made Jesus Lord?

_____

_____

_____

_____

_____

_____

_____

Why did you decide to say yes to Jesus in your teen years?

_____

_____

_____

_____

_____

_____

What has He done in you since you made that decision?

_____

_____

_____

_____

_____

_____

_____

PRAY THE WORD

Thank You, Lord, that 1 Peter 3:15-16 I give honor to You in my heart. As I live for you, if anyone asks about the hope living within me, that I am ready to explain my faith to them with gentleness and respect.

Day 9: Get Your Hopes Up

Return to the stronghold [of security and prosperity] you
prisoners of hope; even today do I declare that I will restore
double your former prosperity to you.
Zechariah 9:12 AMPC

DEVOTIONAL

When you were little, what did you want to be when you "grew up?" As little kids, it's easy for us to dream, but then something happens as we begin to grow up. I think "reality" starts to set in and we think, "How in the world could I do that?" Can I tell you something? God wants you to get your hopes up!

Zechariah 9:12 calls us, "prisoners of hope." Hope isn't wishful thinking. We hear that so much today: "I hope I can go to that event," or "I hope they will call me soon." But, did you know that it is not actually hope, but wishful thinking. Hope is a confident expectation of good. It means that we can be confident that good things are going to happen, because God says they will!

When God is calling us prisoners of hope, He is telling us to get our hopes, our expectancy for good things to happen, up. Become a "prisoner" of always expecting good things to happen in your life. God has nothing but the best in store for us.

However, sometimes it's easier said than done. I was talking to someone the other day who was really struggling to believe God in a certain area of her life. Naturally speaking, there was no way she was going to get out of this situation. It looked hopeless. In those moments, the enemy likes to tell us lies. It's our choice whether or not we are going to stand on the Word of God and be a prisoner of hope, or if we are going to bow down to the enemy and believe his lies. The lie in this situation was that there was no way out of it.

As we talked about the situation, I was able to encourage her not to listen to the enemy's lies, but to stand strong on the Word of God. I gave her several Bible verses to pray and shared with her that this was the time to plant her feet on the ground and not move, because God has already won the victory (Romans 8:37).

God is good. He is faithful. No matter what it looks like on the outside…maybe it's a sickness that you have been fighting off, or maybe it's a challenge at school or at home… whatever it is, get in the Word of God. Find 2 verses to stand on. Plant your feet on that promise and don't move until you win. 1 John 5:4 tells us, "For whatever is born of God overcomes the world. And this is the victory that has overcome the world—our faith." In the end, we win, because of what Jesus Christ has done for us!

CONNECT
Take time to talk to God today. Is there something big that you are believing God for? He wants to provide for you. Ask Him to help you to become a prisoner of hope. When you pray, pray in faith without doubting. When you end your prayer, say, "I believe it and receive it in Jesus' Name." Then choose to believe it and receive it.

TAKE ACTION
What is something big you are believing God for today? Look up Matthew 19:26 and write it down. Now begin to believe that God is coming through for you.

_____

_____

_____

_____

_____

_____

_____

_____

_____

_____

_____

_____

_____

_____

_____

_____

_____

_____

_____

_____

_____

_____

_____

_____

_____

PRAY THE WORD

Thank You, Lord that Zechariah 9:12, that I am a prisoner of hope. I expect good things to happen in my life, because You are the God of security and prosperity.

Day 10: Are You a Problem Solver?

And we know that all things work together for the good of those who love God, to those who are called according to His purpose. For whom He foreknew He also predestined to be conformed to the image of His Son, that He might be firstborn among many brethren. Moreover, whom He predestined these He also called, who He called, these He also justified, these He also glorified.
Romans 8:28-30

DEVOTIONAL

One thing that sets leaders apart from everyone else is that leaders are problem solvers. Instead of just complaining about something that they don't like, they start to think of ways that they can help solve that problem.

Joshua and Caleb were two men in the Bible who were problem solvers. In Numbers 13, God spoke to Moses and told him to send men to spy out the Canaan land, otherwise known as The Promised Land. Out of the 12 men Moses sent out, here was the response of 10 of them in Numbers 13:27-28 after arriving back home, "'We went to the land where you sent us. It truly flows with milk and honey, and this is the fruit. Nevertheless, the people who dwell in the land are strong; the cities are fortified and very large; moreover we saw the descendants of Anak there (the descendants of Anak were giants).'" These guys were scared and started going into all the reasons they could not take Canaan.

However, there were two men who did not see things the way the other men saw them. Numbers 13:30 tells us what Joshua and Caleb thought: "Then Caleb quieted the people before Moses, and said, 'Let us go up at once and take possession, for we are well able to overcome it.'"
Do you see the difference between Joshua and Caleb and the rest of the spies? Joshua and Caleb were ready to go after it. They knew that with God on their side, they could do

anything. However, the other spies were afraid and were making excuse after excuse as to why they were not able to take the land. Numbers 13:33 tells us that these 10 spies actually saw themselves as grasshoppers compared to the people of Canaan. Nothing more than a bug that will get squashed. The 10 spies saw themselves as powerless; therefore, they were powerless.

Joshua and Caleb were different. They saw themselves as confident, strong and able to overcome. Joshua and Caleb knew something that the other spies didn't know. They knew that mountains were meant to be moved. They also knew that to every problem that arises, there is always a solution to overcome it.

The same thing goes for us. When we complain about a problem, we will never get anywhere, but the moment we decide to look to God and His Word and start speaking what God sees instead of what we see, that is the moment we start to gain our victory. We have a choice, we can either call it like we see it or call it like God sees it. It's up to us.

Everyone sees problems. They are all around us if we look hard enough, but it takes courageous people to solve problems.

CONNECT
Is there a problem that you see right now? Have you thought about being a part of the solution? Take time today to talk to God about if this is a problem that He wants you to solve and if so how would He like you to solve it. When you pray, pray in faith without doubting. When you end your prayer, say, "I believe it and receive it in Jesus' Name." Then choose to believe it and receive it.

TAKE ACTION
What is a problem that you have noticed lately? What is one thing you can do to help solve that problem?

_____

_____

_____

_____

_____

_____

_____

_____

_____

_____

_____

_____

_____

_____

_____

_____

_____

_____

_____

_____

PRAY THE WORD

Thank You, Lord, that Romans 8:28-30 all things work together for the good of those who love you and are called according to Your purpose. Thank You for loving me and calling me.

Day 11: Living Out Your Purpose

*Not that I have already attained or am already perfected,
but I press on, that I may lay hold of that for which
Christ Jesus has also laid hold of me.*
Philippians 3:12

DEVOTIONAL

Dreaming can be easy. Acting on those dreams can be scary. Comfort zones are a funny thing, aren't they? They make you feel safe and secure while you're inside of them, but in reality, they're holding you back from being all that God has called you to be. Do you want to know what's even scarier than stepping out of your comfort zone? The thought that if we allow ourselves to stay inside of our comfort zone, the dreams that God has placed in our hearts are dying. It's only when we step out of our comfort zones that our dreams start to come alive.

God doesn't just want you to dream. He wants you to act on your dreams and turn them into reality.

Ecclesiastes 5:3 tells us that dreams come through taking action. It's okay to dream, but if we never take action, what is the point of dreaming in the first place? We will never fulfill our dreams if we don't take the next right step today.

But, how do we take these dreams from dreams and into reality? First things first, we have to take action! What is one small thing we can do today that will bring us closer to achieving those dreams? Is it smiling at someone at the store? Is it making a gift for someone just for fun? Is it writing a chapter in the book you have always wanted to write? Is it learning or making some new recipes that you can share with others? Maybe it's sharing Jesus with someone you know is hurting. Take one small step today.

Colossians 3:23 says, "Whatever you do, do it heartily, as to the Lord and not to men." The reason that we need to do them heartily to the Lord and not to men is because, when we start taking steps toward our dreams, there will be people who will try to stop us. They will criticize what we're doing. They'll make fun of us. However, if we are taking action toward our dreams and we are doing this for the Lord, people can criticize and make fun of us all they want, but they can't stop us.

It's so important to keep pressing on, so others can't steal our God-given dreams from us. This is your dream and not their dream…and if I can be honest, many times they are trying to steal our dreams, because they are afraid to fulfill their own dreams.

The next thing we can do is to stay focused. The root of all failure is broken focus. This can be hard with social media, our friends and school. I'm not saying to neglect those things, but I do encourage you to plan time each day to focus on doing that one next step that will take you closer to your dream. Former president Thomas Jefferson once said, "If you want something you have never had, you must be willing to do something you have never done."

When we focus a little bit of time each day, it's much easier to finish what we start. How many times have you started something and never finished it? To be honest, for me, too many to count. Ecclesiastes 11:4 in the Amplified Classic Version tells us, "He who observes the wind [and waits for all conditions to be favorable] will now sow, and he who regards the clouds will not reap." We can't wait until everything is perfect or think that our life will slow down…it won't. We need to make time to finish what we start so that we can step into our God-given purpose.

And then finally, enjoy the journey! Zechariah 4:10 tells us not to despise the day of small beginnings. Every great victory started with a small first step! Every small win adds up to an even bigger victory. Choose to take the next right step and when you do it, celebrate it! Even if it's just high fiving someone or having a little dance party. Choose to celebrate!

CONNECT

Take time today to talk to God about something you can do today that will help you take steps toward your God-given purpose. Maybe you don't know what that purpose is or maybe you do. There is something we all can do today to make a difference in the lives of those around us. When you pray, pray in faith without doubting. When you end your prayer, say, "I believe it and receive it in Jesus' Name." Then choose to believe it and receive it.

TAKE ACTION

What is something that God has been laying on your heart to do? Is it just to be nicer to people when you're out in public? Is it to write a song or a book? Is it to share your testimony with someone? Write it down, tell a friend or your parents to help hold you accountable and be intentional to make it happen.

_____

_____

_____

_____

_____

_____

_____

_____

_____

_____

_____

_____

_____

_____

_____

_____

_____

_____

_____

_____

_____

_____

_____

_____

_____

_____

_____

_____

_____

_____

PRAY THE WORD

Thank You, Lord, that Philippians 3:12, that I am choosing to press on so that I can fulfill my God-given purpose.

Day 12: Excuses or Results?

Then I said, "Ah, Lord God! Behold, I cannot speak, for I am a youth.' But the Lord said to me, "Do not say, 'I am a youth. For you shall go to all to whom I send you, and whatever I command you, you shall speak. Don't be afraid of their faces, for I am with you to deliver you," says the Lord.
Jeremiah 1:6-8

DEVOTIONAL

Have you ever made an excuse about something because you were too afraid to do it? I have been there more times than I can count. Honestly, I have struggled so many times with the thought, "Who am I to do something like that? I am too shy"...or "I am not an expert"...or whatever other excuse I could come up with. If you have ever had those thoughts, you are not alone. Jeremiah, who had a whole book of the Bible written about him, was right there, too.

Let's look at Jeremiah's response to God when God explained to Jeremiah what his purpose was: Jeremiah 1:6, "Ah, Lord God! Behold, I cannot speak, for I am a youth." Excuses are so funny. I'm 100 percent sure that when God called Jeremiah, God knew how old he was. Jeremiah's response was basically, "Uh, God! I don't think so. Don't you know how old I am? I'm too young to make a difference. I don't know what to say. I'm too afraid to do it. What if they reject me? There are people out there who are way more qualified than I am." I can almost see 17-year-old Jeremiah start to freak out a little bit.

Know that God has created you for a specific purpose. When He calls you, He knows what He's doing. Yes, stepping out can be scary. When God calls us, He calls us to something so much bigger than ourselves. The reason why is because if we could do it in our own strength, we wouldn't need God.

Jeremiah 1:7-8 says, "But the Lord said to me, 'Do not say, 'I am a youth.' For you shall go to all to whom I send you, and whatever I command you, you shall speak. Do not be afraid of their faces, for I am with you to deliver you.'" God is saying, "Don't worry, I am not going to leave you alone. When I call you to do something big, I will show you what steps to take, I will tell you what words to say. I am there with you.

I want to specifically point out verse 8 where God says, "Do not be afraid of their faces, for I am with you." Have you ever been afraid to do something that you know you should do or maybe even something you wanted to do, but you didn't because you were afraid of what others were going to think about you? Honestly, when we don't step out, that is the underlying fear of why we don't whether we realize it or not. That is exactly what this verse is talking about. God is going to deliver you from being stuck inside of the head of other people. So many times we think, "What if I fail?" or "What if they laugh at me?" God is telling us that we don't have to worry about that.

Can I be honest with you? The majority of people are not even worried about you. They are worried about the same thing you are—what people are going to think about them.

CONNECT
What is something God has been talking to you about doing that you haven't done yet? Talk to God about it and thank Him for giving you courage to do it (Joshua 1:5). When you pray, pray in faith without doubting. When you end your prayer, say, "I believe it and receive it in Jesus' Name." Then choose to believe it and receive it.

TAKE ACTION
What is one thing that you are going to do today that scares you? I'm not talking about a roller coaster or climb up 20 flights of stairs. What is one thing that God has been telling

you to do that you haven't done, yet. Choose to step out knowing that God is with you.

_____

_____

_____

_____

_____

_____

_____

_____

_____

_____

_____

_____

_____

_____

_____

_____

_____

PRAY THE WORD

Thank you, Lord, that Jeremiah 1:7-8, I will not make excuses to hold myself back from what you have called me to do. I will choose to trust that You are with me, guiding my steps.

Day 13: Confident Faith

*If anyone longs to be wise, ask God for wisdom and
He will give it. He won't see your lack of wisdom as an
opportunity to scold you over your failures,
but He will overwhelm your failures with His generous grace.
Just make sure you ask empowered by confident faith
without doubting that you will receive.*
James 1:5-6 TPT

DEVOTIONAL

You may be thinking, "I have no clue what God has called me to do with my life." The truth is, even those of us who are walking in God's plan for our life don't truly know all that God has called us to do, so don't feel alone. It starts with taking one step at a time.

Discovering our purpose is a journey. It's not actually something we just decide, it's actually something that we get to discover as we continue to walk out that journey. If you are feeling clueless, it's okay! Ask God to show you what He wants you to do today…what you can do right now. Start there. The key is making the next right decision.

Our life is a path that consists of the choices that we make. Psalm 16:11 says, "You (The Lord) will show me the path of life; in Your presence is fullness of joy, at Your right hand there are pleasures forevermore." When we take the steps that lead us down the path God has laid out for us, we get to live out an abundant life of fullness and joy!

But how do we really know if the steps that we are taking are the ones that God has called us to take? This was something that I struggled with for quite some time after I became a Christian. I would always second guess myself: "Is it God speaking to me or is it just because I want it that way?"

Habakkuk 2:1 says, "I will stand my watch and set myself on the rampart and watch and see what He will say to me, and what I will answer when I am corrected." The first way to position ourselves to hear from God is to watch for God to speak to us. We do this by spending time with God daily in praise, in prayer and reading His Word.

When you spend time with God daily, keep a look out for what God is saying to you. When you pray, be sure to not always do the talking, but take time to listen to God as well. When you're reading the Bible, take time to think about what you're reading and how you can apply it to your life. The primary way that God speaks to us is through His Word. That's why it's so important to not just read it to check off something on your to-do list, but to connect with God.

Now, moving on, Habakkuk 2:2 tells us to, "Write the vision and make it plain on tablets, that he may run who reads it." When God speaks to you, grab an empty notebook or a journal and write it down. Make this a place that you go to often so that you remember what He's saying to you.

Know that when God tells you something or you read one of His promises in the Bible, He will make it happen. Finally, in Habakkuk 2:3, we read, "For the vision is yet for an appointed time; but at the end it will speak, and it will not lie. Though it tarries, wait for it; because it will surely come, it will not tarry." That word tarry is a fancy word for "It may take longer than you think." It may take time for you to see His promise, because He might need to prepare you for when it comes. So, don't get discouraged if you don't see it right away. It's coming.

CONNECT
Take time today to talk to God about what He wants to say to you. Ask Him to help you hear Him. When you pray, pray in faith without doubting. When you end your prayer, say, "I believe it and receive it in Jesus' Name." Then choose to believe it and receive it.

TAKE ACTION

Today, I encourage you to take 15 minutes to spend alone with God. Go ahead and put your devices in airplane mode, set an alarm for 15 minutes. On the next page, the empty one, write down everything that comes to your mind—no matter what it is. This is called a brain dump.

At first, this is going to be really easy—a lot of thoughts will come to mind (usually things you need to do, could be doing, or forgot to do). Write all of those thoughts down. After about the 5 minute mark, it will start to get tough, but don't give up. Keep pushing through.

What you are doing is allowing all the stuff that has been clouding your mind to get out and opening yourself up to allowing God to speak into your heart. After about 10 minutes, you may be thinking, "Why am I doing this?" That's okay, keep writing your thoughts down. It's in these moments where Psalm 46:10 comes to life, "Be still and know that I am God."

After 15 minutes, look at what you wrote down. What was God speaking to your heart today?

PRAY THE WORD

Thank You, Lord, that in James 1:5, you tell us that if anyone lacks wisdom, that you will give it to them freely. Thank You for showing me what you are saying to me today.

Day 14: God Confidence

I have strength for all things in Christ Who empowers me
[I am ready for anything and equal to anything
through Him Who infuses inner strength into me;
I am self-sufficient in Christ's sufficiency.]
Philippians 4:13 AMPC

DEVOTIONAL

One thing that I love about God is that He is a big God and when He does things, He does them in a big way. Did you know that the book of Philippians in the New Testament is called the "Book of Joy?" Paul talks a lot about joy in Philippians. What you may not know, though is that Paul actually wrote this book when he was in prison. This is a bit gross, but where Paul was in prison was also the same place where all of the sewage ran off into. Paul was probably knee deep in sewage and yet he still took the time to write a book about joy.

Why? Because Paul knew something that he wanted to share with everyone. Philippians 4:13 says, "I can do all things through Christ who strengthens me." He knew that His strength came from the Lord and he wants you to know that your strength comes from the Lord, too.

Nehemiah 8:10 tells us that the joy of the Lord is where we get our strength. Joy means that there is dance party going on inside of you at all times. You may think of happiness when you think of joy, but actually joy and happiness are two very different things.

So what is happiness? Happiness is based on everything going on around us...our circumstances. When things are going great, it's easy to be happy. But, when things aren't going so well, it's not always easy to be happy. Our circumstances are always changing, they may be up one minute and down the next.

Unlike happiness, joy is based on the Lord and not on the circumstances around us. God, unlike our circumstances, never changes. He is good all the time. Joy is knowing that even though things aren't going great right now, I have a peace on the inside of me, because I know my God has my back on this. Joy keeps going even when things are tough.

Have you ever met someone who had something tragic happen to them, yet they seem so calm? They aren't hysterical, like so many others would be. There is something about them that's different. That's joy…and that's where we find our strength. Joy is not a feeling, but it is a choice. It was given to us as a fruit of the Spirit when we became a Christian (Galatians 5:22-23), but in order to grow our joy, we have to choose it. As we choose to believe God and His Word over the circumstances, that's when joy begins to grow.

God has called you to do big things for Him and it can be scary and uncomfortable. That is where the joy of the Lord that's inside of you comes in handy. God wants to use you to bless so many people and He is with you the whole way.

CONNECT
Take time today to thank God for putting His joy on the inside of you. Ask Him to help you choose joy when times get tough. When you pray, pray in faith without doubting. When you end your prayer, say, "I believe it and receive it in Jesus' Name." Then choose to believe it and receive it.

TAKE ACTION
What does the Word say about joy?

Nehemiah 8:10

_____

_____

Philippians 4:13

_____

_____

_____

_____

Romans 15:13

_____

_____

_____

_____

Philemon 1:7

_____

_____

_____

_____

PRAY THE WORD
Thank You, Lord that Nehemiah 8:10, that the joy of the Lord is my strength!

Part 3:
Dare to…
Lead

Day 1: Created to Make a Difference

*Now when they saw the boldness of Peter and John,
and perceived that they were uneducated and untrained
men, they marveled. And they realized
that they had been with Jesus.*
Acts 4:13

WORD STUDY

UNEDUCATED: Greek Word: agrammatos

Peter and John were not scholars. They didn't take
classes in the Jewish schools. They were common
people, not professionals.

DEVOTIONAL

Did you know that anyone who wants to be used by God can
be! It's not a question of whether or not God wants to use us
to do incredible things, but whether or not we want God to
use us. God's not looking to see if you are qualified to do
something or if you are the best at something. All He's
looking for is if you are available for Him to use you.

1 Corinthians 1:27-29 says, "But God has chosen the foolish
things of the world to put to shame the wise and God has
chosen the weak things of the world to put to shame the
things which are mighty; and the base things of the world
and the things which are despised God has chosen, and the
things which are not, to bring to nothing the things that are,
that no flesh should glory in His presence."

Even if we aren't the smartest person, the most talented
person, or even the strongest person, that's great news,
because we are the one God wants. He tells us in these
verses that He has chosen the foolish things of the world to
put to shame the wise. That word, "foolish" is the Greek
word, "mōros." We get the English word moron from this

word. He says, that even if we aren't the smartest person alive, He can use us put to shame the wise. That means that God is going to cause us to stand out in a crowd in a good way. He is going to raise us up to be a leader among people.

Acts 4:13 says, "Now when they (the crowd) saw the boldness of Peter and John, and perceived that they were uneducated and untrained men, they marveled. And they realized that they had been with Jesus." Peter and John were not scholars or professional speakers. They didn't go to the best schools. They were common people like us that allowed God to use them. I love this, because even though there was nothing out of the ordinary about them, they were common men and yet the people still marveled They knew something was different about them and what they saw was what was different was their relationship with Jesus.

God is saying right now, it doesn't matter what other people think about you. It doesn't matter if you are the smartest person alive. I still choose you! God wants to use you to be a leader for Him so that He can use you to make an impact for His kingdom. He wants to use you to be a world changer! God wants to use common people like you and me.

CONNECT
Take time today to thank God for choosing you to do incredible things for His kingdom. What an incredible honor! When you pray, be sure pray in faith without doubting. When you end your prayer, say, "I believe it and receive it in Jesus' Name." Then choose to believe it and receive it.

TAKE ACTION
God wants to use you today. What is one thing that you can do to make a difference in the life of someone around you today?

_____

_____

_____

_____

_____

_____

_____

_____

_____

_____

_____

_____

_____

_____

_____

_____

_____

_____

_____

_____

_____

PRAY THE WORD

Thank You, Lord, that Acts 4:13, just like Peter and John, even though I am a common person, you are using me to make a major impact in the lives of others because of my relationship with you.

Day 2: Character is the Key

An inheritance gained hastily at the beginning
will not be blessed at the end.
Proverbs 20:21

DEVOTIONAL

Have you ever met those people who just seem like they can always draw in a crowd…like no matter where they are, people just flock to them? They have charisma bursting at the seams. They are magnetic.

I remember the summer after my senior year in high school. I was getting ready to go to college and I had it all planned out. See, in high school, I was known for being shy and quiet. I would sit on the sidelines and watch everyone else wishing I were them. I didn't have much confidence in who I was.

Well, the summer after my senior year in high school, I decided that I was going to go to college and I was going to act like that person I always wanted to be…the one who could walk in a room and draw a crowd. I was going to introduce myself to everyone I saw. No one knew me so I thought that without a shadow of a doubt I could become anyone that I wanted to be…right? I mean, people say all the time, "You can do anything you put your mind to." I had my mind made up and it seemed so simple. However, that's not who God created me to be. I did meet some pretty neat people that I would not have met otherwise. One of them even became my best friend throughout college, but it didn't quite work out the way I thought it would. After the initial excitement, I was done.

Charisma is great at drawing crowds, but character is what will keep them there. What I didn't realize is that if I wanted to be used by God in a way that was going to make a difference for Him, it wasn't my charisma that I needed to work on, but my character.

I have met charismatic people in my life that have great character. However, I have met some charismatic people who do not have any character at all. These people are good with drawing crowds, but there was no depth to them. They would make promises and never follow through on them. You couldn't count on them for anything, because half the time they would forget and not show up.

Charismatic people who lack character like things easy. They want to just walk into a room and have everything done for them, but they are not people who make good leaders, because the moment things get hard, they will quit. People who have character will push through when things get hard. They will not quit until they see the end goal accomplished.

What is character? What does it look like? Godly character includes things like integrity and walking in love.

What is integrity? Integrity means that we are choosing to do the right thing when nobody else is doing it. It is doing the right thing when you are alone. It is making the right decision even when it's hard to make.

As for the love, Romans 5:5 says that the love of God has been poured out in our hearts by the Holy Spirit. God has given us His love so that we can love others. Walking in love includes things like speaking well of others instead of tearing them down. It includes encouraging others and building them up. It includes praying for others that you know are hurting. It includes looking for ways to bless others and to serve them.

Building your character is way more important than drawing a crowd. It's way more important than any gift or talent God has given you. If you don't have character, you cannot make a lasting impact in the lives of others. You might make an impact for a short while, but it will not last long.

CONNECT

Take time today to talk to God about your character. Ask Him what areas He would like you to grow in. When you pray, be sure pray in faith without doubting. When you end your prayer, say, "I believe it and receive it in Jesus' Name." Then choose to believe it and receive it.

TAKE ACTION

Write down what integrity means. Are you walking in integrity in all areas of your life? If not, start today to make the next right decision.

Integrity is:

_____

_____

_____

_____

_____

Integrity is:

_____

_____

_____

_____

_____

Integrity is:

_____

_____

_____

_____

_____

Integrity is:

_____

_____

_____

_____

_____

PRAY THE WORD

Thank You Lord, that Romans 5:5 Your love has been poured out in my heart by the Holy Spirit so that I can love others the way that you love them.

Day 3: The Ultimate Secret of Success

But seek first the kingdom of God and His righteousness,
and all these things shall be added to you.
Matthew 6:33

DEVOTIONAL

I recently went online and did a search on what the top successful people in the world thought was the ultimate secret to success was and what I found sounded like great things. One person said a positive mindset. Another person said you had to have a belief in yourself and what you are doing. Another one said that you needed to be bold. Yet another one said the key is in reading books. And the last one said, the key is in taking action. Now don't get me wrong, all of these things are great and to be a great leader, it does take doing all of these things. However, none of these things are what is considered the ultimate secret of success.

The ultimate secret of success is actually found in your alone time with God. Before God will ever raise you up to give you a platform, we must develop a strong relationship with God in our private life first. Are we choosing to put God first in every area of our life? It's in the areas where we put Him first that become the most blessed. Are we choosing to put God first in the mornings? When we do, over time, we will see that our life will be blessed. Are we putting God first in our friendships or our relationships? If so, that area of your life over time will be blessed.

In 1 Kings 17:8-16 we see a story about Elijah when God asked him to visit a poor widow. God had just given Elijah word to go to Zarephath and as soon as he arrived there, he saw the widow gathering sticks. He went up to her and asked her if she could bring him a cup of water and a piece of the bread that was in her hand. Verse 12 says, "So she said, 'As the Lord your God lives, I do not have bread, only a handful of flour in a bin, and a little oil in a jar; and see, I am gathering a couple of sticks that I may go in and prepare it for myself and my son, that we may eat it, and die.'" This widow's life was a mess. She was broken and hurting and ready to give up on life. She had no hope.

Now going on to verse 13 it says, "And Elijah said to her, "Do not fear; go and do as you have said, but make me a small cake from it first, and bring it to me; and afterward make some for yourself and your son." If we stop there, what Elijah just said this widow, it sounds like he wants her to give him food first and if there was anything left over, that's what she should feed her and her son. It almost sounds selfish, right?

But God was trying to show this widow a promise that He had for her. He knew that whatever area of her life that she put God first in, it would eventually be blessed. This lady was struggling in every way and God wanted to take care of her, yet she wasn't letting Him, because she wasn't putting Him first. Elijah came along to help her see that.

Let's keep reading in verse 14, Elijah talking, "For thus says the Lord God of Israel: "The bin of flour shall not be used up, nor shall the jar of oil run dry, until the day the Lord sends rain on the earth." How incredible is that? Because she chose to put God first, she now has a bin of flour that even if she uses the slightest bit, it will be continually refilled. She will also have a jar of oil that will never run dry.

Basically, what God is trying to tell this widow through Elijah is, "Don't give up hope. If you put Me first in your life, I will provide for you and I will give you all that you need and more!" Just like with the widow, whatever area you put God first in your life, will be the area that is the most blessed.

CONNECT
The ultimate secret to success is found in your private time with God. Take time today to talk to God. Is there an area of your life that you have been holding back from God? Ask Him. If so, He will reveal it in the right time. When you pray,

be sure pray in faith without doubting. When you end your prayer, say, "I believe it and receive it in Jesus' Name." Then choose to believe it and receive it.

TAKE ACTION

Are you putting God first in every area of your life? Is there an area that you have been holding back from God? Or maybe it's even that you get distracted in your alone time with Him. Write it down with an action plan to help hold yourself accountable.

_____

_____

_____

_____

_____

_____

_____

_____

_____

_____

_____

_____

_____

_____

PRAY THE WORD

Thank You, Lord, that Matthew 6:33, as I seek first Your kingdom and Your righteousness, You provide the most blessed life for me. Thank You for taking care of me and providing for all my needs.

Day 4: Choose Your Friends Wisely

*Do you want to be a mighty warrior? It's better to be
known as one who is patient and slow to anger.
Do you want to conquer a city? Rule over your temper
before you attempt to rule a city.*
Proverbs 16:32 TPT

DEVOTIONAL

"Discipline is choosing between what you want now and
what you want most." Abraham Lincoln

Sometimes in life we have to make decisions that are really
hard. The decisions that we make today are connected to
where we will end up in our future. When we make the right
choices, it will lead us closer to our God-given dreams.
When we make the wrong choices, it will lead us further
away from our God-given dreams. Because living out our
purpose is quite a few years out, we don't always think about
the importance of our decisions today and how it directly
reflects our future.

I think one of the hardest decisions that we will ever make in
life, both in the teen years and the adult years, is choosing
who our friends will be. I think this is especially hard for
teens, because a lot of your friends you've known since you
were in kindergarten or before. However, as you get older,
some of your friends might begin to make decisions that are
not good. I will tell you, this is when decision-making is hard,
but absolutely necessary.

Have you heard the saying, "Show me your three closest
friends and I will show you your future?" The truth is,
eventually we become like the people we hang around. If
you really want to know what your future will look like, look at
the three to five friends who you are the closest to. Are they
a picture of what you want your future to look like? Are they
a picture of someone you want to be like? If not, I encourage

you to choose differently.

It's a lot harder to bring someone up to where you are in your walk with God than it is for them to pull you down to their level. Think about it this way: you are standing on a platform and your friend, the one not making the greatest decisions, is below you on the ground. If you were to reach out and grab their hand, would it be easier to pull them up to the platform with you or will it be easier for them to pull you down to the floor. Thanks to a little thing called gravity, it is going to be a whole lot easier for them to pull you down. The same thing is true for life.

Proverbs 13:20 says, "He who walks with wise men will be wise, but the companion of fools will be destroyed." Notice, this verse doesn't say that a fool will be destroyed, but the companion or friend of fools is the one who will be destroyed.

If you are struggling to find friends that love God and want to make a difference for Him, talk to Him about it. I promise you; you are not the only Christian who wants to have a strong walk with God. Ask God to bring you the right friends…friends who have good morals, good character, good attitudes and good friends themselves…friends who love the Lord and want to make a difference for Him with you. You may not see these new friends over night, but over time, God will bring them to you. However, I encourage you, from the moment you ask God to bring you those friends, continue to thank Him for it every day until you see it happen. They are coming!

Craig Groeschel, Pastor of Life Church says, "It is impossible for you to live the right life when you have the wrong friends."

CONNECT
God has nothing but the best in store for you. Take time today to talk to God about the friends that you have. Ask Him to bring you Godly friends who love Him, who have good

character, good attitudes, good morals and good friends themselves. When you pray, be sure to pray in faith without doubting. When you end your prayer, say, "I believe it and receive it in Jesus' Name." Then choose to believe it and receive it.

TAKE ACTION

Make a list of your three closest friends. After each friend, answer these questions about them: What are they most interested in? What kind of words do they use? Do they encourage others or tear others down? What kinds of movies or shows do they watch? Where do they hang out on online? Then ask yourself, "are they a good friend?" If they are, circle their name. If not, it's time to pray for them and move on.

Friend #1: _____

- *Are the things they're interested in bringing them closer to God or taking them away from Him?* _____

  _____

- *Do their words encourage others or tear them down?*

  _____

  _____

- Are the shows they watch and the sites they visit something God would approve of? _____

  _____

Friend #2: _____
- *Are the things they're interested in bringing them closer to God or taking them away from Him?* _____

  _____

• *Do their words encourage others or tear them down?*

_____

_____

• Are the shows they watch and the sites they visit something God would approve of? _____

_____

Friend #3: _____

• *Are the things they're interested in bringing them closer to God or taking them away from Him?* _____

_____

• *Do their words encourage others or tear them down?*

_____

_____

• Are the shows they watch and the sites they visit something God would approve of? _____

_____

PRAY THE WORD

Thank You, Lord, that Proverbs 13:20, when I choose to walk with wise friends, friends who love you and want to make a difference for you, I will be wise myself.

Day 5: Compassion is Critical

*Finally, all of you be of one mind, having compassion
for one another; love as brothers (or sisters),
be tenderhearted, be courteous;*
1 Peter 3:8

DEVOTIONAL

"A true leader has the confidence to stand alone, the courage to make tough decisions, and the compassion to listen to the needs of others." Douglas MacAurthur

In order to be compassionate, we need to really understand what compassion is. So many times we confuse compassion with sympathy when actually they are really two very different things.

Sympathy is a feeling of pity or sorrow for something bad that has happened for someone else. Since sympathy is a feeling, we see that it is based on our emotions. Sympathy is basically saying, "Awe, I hate that happened to you. I'm so sorry you are walking through that."

Compassion is having that feeling of sympathy toward someone, but it doesn't stop there. Compassion is a desire from deep inside of us to do something to help that person. Compassion moves us to action. So, where sympathy is just a feeling, compassion says, "What can I do to help you?"

I love getting to see the life of Jesus as He walked on this earth. Jesus lived a life of compassion. Matthew 9:36 says, "But when He (Jesus) saw the multitudes, He was moved with compassion for them, because they were weary and scattered, like sheep having no shepherd." See, when Jesus started his ministry, He watched people. As He was walking through the crowds, He would notice that the people all around Him were hurting and had no hope. This verse says they were like sheep without a shepherd, just walking around aimlessly with no vision for a future.

However, Jesus didn't just see them and feel the pain of the people, He chose to step up and step into that role of a Shepherd. His mission was to tell everyone about our incredible Heavenly Father and how much He loved them. He wanted to give them vision where there was none before. He wanted to give them hope where there was none before. He wanted to heal the people where they were hurting and broken and He did just that.

Many times on Wednesday nights, as a youth leader, I stand back and watch the students in our youth ministry. Some of them are on fire for God and others, not so much. I look at the ones who haven't decided to go all in with Jesus and I see the sadness in their eyes. I see the pain, the loneliness and the hurting. However, just like Jesus, I don't just sympathize with them and do nothing about it; I take action. What I do when I see these youth is first, I start to imagine those same youth as if they received a revelation of how much God loves them and how hope now fills their eyes. It gets me so excited and honestly, that is what moves me to compassion. That's why I am a part of youth ministry, so I can be a part of them receiving that revelation. I know what those hurting and broken teenagers were like. I was there as a teen. It wasn't until a friend of mine invited me to church where I heard the Good News of Jesus and my life was completely changed. That's what I want for those youth.

God understands the depth of our hurt and our pain. His compassion sees beyond the feelings and the emotions and since He lives on the inside of us, we are able to see things from His perspective. That's when He moves us to action.

I will be completely honest and tell you that loving others was tough for me at first. I mean, I was kind to others, but when it came to giving hugs or telling people I loved them, that was tough for me, because I didn't grow up in a loving environment. You may be thinking, "How do I love others or how do I move with compassion like Jesus did to where I can make a big difference?" You may be facing some real fears when it comes to reaching out to other teens and sharing the love of Jesus with them.

Well, I have good news for you. Romans 5:5 tells us that the love of God has been poured out in our hearts by the Holy Spirit. You have God's love on the inside of you to love others with. You don't have to do it on your own! 1 John 4:18-19 says, "There is no fear in love, but perfect love casts out all fear, because fear involves torment. But he who fears has not been made perfect in love. We love Him, because He first loved us." Basically, what that's saying is, "if you are afraid, don't get upset or think poorly about yourself, just dig into verses on how much God loves you. Find verses that have to do with God's love for you and speak them over yourself daily until you feel that fear leave. Perfect love casts out all fear. It has to go!

CONNECT

Take time today to ask God to help you see others through His eyes. When you do, and you ask Him from your heart, He will start to show you people around you that you can start to make a difference for. When you pray, be sure to pray in faith without doubting. When you end your prayer, say, "I believe it and receive it in Jesus' Name." Then choose to believe it and receive it.

TAKE ACTION

As you begin to notice the people around you, allow yourself to be moved with compassion to do something to help them. It could be something as simple as opening the door for someone when you go up to a building or helping a mom at church who has her hands full. When you take action, be sure to write below what you did.

_____

_____

_____

_____

_____

_____

_____

_____

_____

_____

_____

_____

_____

_____

_____

_____

_____

_____

_____

_____

_____

_____

PRAY THE WORD

Thank You, Lord, that 1 Peter 3:8, Lord I have the same compassion Jesus did when He walked on this earth. Thank You, Lord, that I love others, I am tenderhearted, and I am courteous to others.

Day 6: Keep the Vision in Front of You

But Jesus said to him, "No one, having put his hand to the plow, and looking back, is fit for the kingdom of God.
Luke 9:62

DEVOTIONAL

Vision is more than just setting goals. It's more than dreaming. Having a vision gives you the ability to see what you want in the future while using the wisdom God has given you.

Having a vision is like having a GPS when you are on a long road trip. Imagine that your parents just received a phone call, and it turns out that they were heirs of this incredible property in the Rocky Mountains. This property comes with an amazing house and a heated indoor pool. It comes with horses and horse trails. The problem is, the attorney on the other end of the phone has no idea what the address is or even what city and state this property is in. All he knows is that it's in the Rocky Mountains. The Rocky Mountains cover nine different states. How likely will it be that you will be able to find your family's new property? Not very likely, right? You don't have an address. You don't have even a city or a state, let alone the directions on how to get there.

This is exactly what happens when we've set a goal for our life, but don't have a vision on how to get there. God has a specific purpose for each and every one of us, but if we don't have a plan of how to get there, we aren't going to fulfill that purpose. The decisions and choices we make today will directly affect whether or not we reach that purpose. Unfortunately, we won't just wake up there in a couple years by accident if we don't make the right choices today. It's just like we won't get to that incredible property in the Rocky Mountains just by driving aimlessly. We need to have a plan; a roadmap to get us there.

Proverbs 29:18 tells us, "Where there is no revelation (or vision), the people cast off restraint." Or in other words, they limit themselves from what God can do in their lives. When we don't have a vision, we will never be able to accomplish the dream that God has for us. That dream then will begin to die and we won't be as effective for the Lord. Vision creates hope. It brings change. You were created to be a world changer, a difference maker!

Habakkuk 2:2 says, "Then the Lord answered me and said, "Write the vision and make it plain on tablets, that he may run who reads it."

That is exactly what a vision does! After God shows you your vision, you need keep it in front of you so that you can run toward your God-given purpose each and every day.

But, how do we keep our vision in front of us according to Habakkuk?

1.Write the vision down
2.Make it plain (or clear)
3.Make sure it will motivate you

When thinking about your vision, ask yourself these questions:

1. What does a successful person's friends look like?

2. What does a successful person's family relationships look like?

3. What does a successful person's relationship with God look like?

4. What do successful friends look like for you?

5. What does a successful family relationship look like for you?

6. What does a successful relationship with God look like to you?

119

When you have answered these questions and gotten really clear on them, write them down. Then, find a picture to print or to cut out that reminds you of each of those answers. Put them on a cork board or on the front of a notebook where you will see it often...or even the home screen of your phone. Keep that vision in front of you to help you keep running toward your dream so that you can fulfill your God-given purpose.

CONNECT

Take time today to talk to God about each of the questions above. Ask Him to help you answer these questions. When you pray, be sure pray in faith without doubting. When you end your prayer, say, "I believe it and receive it in Jesus' Name." Then choose to believe it and receive it.

TAKE ACTION

Take some time to answer these questions. Really think about them.

1. **What does a successful person's friends look like? Is this what your friends look like?**

   _____

   _____

   _____

   _____

   _____

   _____

   _____

2. **What does a successful person's family relationships look like? Is this what your relationship with your family looks like?**

   _____

_____

_____

_____

_____

_____

_____

3. **What does a successful person's relationship with God look like? Is this what your relationship with God looks like?**

_____

_____

_____

_____

_____

_____

_____

If not, don't beat yourself up. Circle one of these areas that you can start working on to align yourself up with what success looks like.

PRAY THE WORD

Thank You, Lord, that Ephesians 3:20, by your power that is at work within me, I am able to carry out your purpose for my life and do superabundantly far over and above all that we dare ask or think and infinitely beyond my highest prayers, desires, thoughts hopes and dreams.

Day 7: Pray and Take Action

Every one of the builders had his sword girded at
his side as he built. And the one who sounded
the trumpet was beside me.
Nehemiah 4:18

DEVOTIONAL

Dream thieves....is there really such a thing? If so, what are they? Dream thieves are real. They are people who will try hard to pull you off of the course that will lead you to your purpose. Nehemiah had them in his life, Joseph had them in his life, Jesus had them in His life, and we will have them in our lives as well. It's up to us to not let them steal our God-given dream.

I heard my pastor, Jim Frease, say this and it stuck with me, "When God wants to bless you, He will use people. When the devil wants to curse you, he will use people." God uses us to bless the lives of others, however, the devil uses people as well to curse others. This is why it is so important to surround ourselves with people who are going to support our dreams, not try to steal them from us.

Joseph was a prime example of someone who had dream thieves. Now, Joseph didn't surround himself with people who were going to build him up. He surrounded himself with his brothers who were already jealous of him. In Genesis 37:3, we see that Joseph was his father's favorite son. That could not have been easy for his brothers to swallow.

So, think about how Joseph's brothers felt when one day Joseph goes up to them and tells them about a dream he just had. In this dream, he dreamt that one day his brothers would bow down to him and serve him. In Genesis 37:8, we see his brothers weren't so happy about that, "And his brothers said to him, "Shall you indeed reign over us? Or shall you indeed have dominion over us?" So they hated him even more for his dreams and for his words." As if that wasn't enough, Joseph had yet another dream and because he didn't learn from it the first time, he decided to tell his brothers a second dream. In this dream, it was the same kind of thing: one day his brothers would bow to him and serve him. This made the brothers irate.

These brothers had such a hatred for Joseph that we see in Genesis 37, that they actually conspired to kill him. But thankfully, Reuben was there. In Genesis 37:21, Reuben encouraged his brothers not to kill Joseph out right, but to throw him into a deep pit. Then, after his brothers were gone, Reuben was going to come back and help Joseph out of the pit. But before they went through with that plan, his brothers thought about it some more. Genesis 37:26-27 says, " So Judah said to his brothers, 'What profit *is there* if we kill our brother and conceal his blood? Come and let us sell him to the Ishmaelites, and let not our hand be upon him, for he *is* our brother *and* our flesh.' And his brothers listened."

From there, they sold Joseph in Egypt to Potiphar, who was one of Pharaoh's top officials. While in Potiphar's house, Joseph encountered his next dream thief...Potiphar's wife. Genesis 38 tells us that Potiphar's wife lied about Joseph concerning some pretty serious accusations. Then in Genesis 38:20, because of the accusations, Joseph was thrown into jail. Joseph could have given up, but he didn't, he kept his eyes on his vision. Joseph stayed true to His walk with God. He chose to trust God and kept pursuing his dreams until he prospered right where he was in prison.

Eventually, Joseph was able to get out of prison and in Genesis 41, Joseph was raised to power and became second in command to Pharaoh. This is where Joseph's dreams began to come true and his brothers did end up serving Joseph.

One question you might ask is, "How did Joseph stay so strong through all of the challenges he faced?" "How did he not give up or back down?" The answer, Joseph kept his vision in front of him and he stayed focused on it.

All failure is a result of broken focus. We do not fail at anything unless we take our eyes off of the end result. Just because we stumble, doesn't mean we have to quit. It just means we need to get back up and try again. I think of Thomas Edison when he created the lightbulb. He didn't create the light bulb the first time he tried or even the 100th time he tried. He would not take his focus off of his end goal. In the end, he said, "I didn't fail. I just found 2,000 ways not to make a lightbulb; I only need to find one way to make it work."

Negative attacks will come our way, but we don't need to give in to them. The enemy wants nothing more than to make you ineffective for the kingdom of God. He wants to get you off of your calling, attack your identity and pull you down. So be like Nehemiah in Nehemiah 4:18 and fight with one hand (through prayer) and take action with the other.

CONNECT
Take time today to ask God if you are on the right track to fulfilling your purpose. Talk to Him about what He wants you to do today to make the next right decision to stay on that track. When you pray, be sure pray in faith without doubting. When you end your prayer, say, "I believe it and receive it in Jesus' Name." Then choose to believe it and receive it.

TAKE ACTION
Take time today to journal. Write down your thoughts concerning today's devotions and previous devotions that stand out to you. It's okay to just write out what comes to your mind.

_____

_____

_____

_____

_____

_____

_____

_____

_____

_____

_____

_____

_____

_____

_____

_____

_____

_____

_____

_____

_____

_____

PRAY THE WORD

Thank You, Lord, that Nehemiah 4:18, I will choose to go after my dreams no matter what. Through prayer and taking action, I will fulfill my God-given purpose.

Day 8: Obedience without Compromise

But Jesus said, "More than that, blessed are those who hear the word of God and keep it!"
Luke 11:28

WORD STUDY
BLESSED: Greek Word: Makarios

Supremely blessed, fortunate, well off, happy

DEVOTIONAL

It's a trend now more than ever to compromise on the Word of God in order to reach people. I have seen pastors going away from teaching the Bible to only teaching feel good messages. I have heard of praise and worship bands mixing in popular secular music during their praise and worship and even at youth events in order to be relevant to today's teens. However, it is so important to never compromise on the Word of God when it comes to reaching people.

Now, I'm not saying that pastors should be standing up on stage yelling at everyone that they are going to hell. That's not Biblical and it's not going to reach very many people. I'm not saying that praise and worship bands should hang up their hats, pull out the organs and hymnals and start singing hymn 101. Some churches still do that, I get it. There is nothing wrong with hymns, but they probably aren't going to be relevant to teens today, right?

When reaching out to others who have not given their life to the Lord, it is so important not to compromise on the Word of God order to reach them. Yes, we want to be relevant, but we cannot compromise on the Word of God. If we do compromise on what the Bible says, people who don't know Jesus will never see the hope in us that they need. They don't yet realize they have a need that only the Savior can give them.

In I Corinthians 9:19-22 it says, "For although I am free in every way from anyone's control, I have made myself a bond servant to everyone, so that I might gain the more [for Christ]. To the Jews I became as a Jew, that I might win Jews; to men under the Law, [I became] as one under the Law, though (I myself am not) under the Law, that I might win those under the Law. To those without (outside) law I became as one without law, not that I am without the law of God…but that I am [especially keeping] within *and* committed to the law of Christ, that I might win those who are without law. To the weak…I have become… that I might win the weak…I have [in short] become all things to all men, that I might by all means (at all costs and in any and every way) save some [by winning them to faith in Jesus Christ].

Basically, what Paul is saying in these verses is that in order to reach people for Jesus, he couldn't compromise on the Word of God, but he did have to find common ground with them. For the Jews, Paul could relate, because he was a Jew. He understood where they came from. It doesn't mean he became a Jew or he acted like a Jew, but that he could find common ground, because he was once there and now he gained freedom in Christ.

That's what we must do to reach people. We need to find common ground. The only way to find common ground is to ask them questions. What school do they go to? Do they play music or like to draw? What activities do they enjoy? Do they like a certain movie? People always want to talk about what they are passionate about.

CONNECT
Take time to talk to God today about who it is that He wants you to reach. Ask him to give you the Words to speak so that you aren't compromising on the Word of God, but instead finding common ground. When you pray, be sure to pray in

faith without doubting. When you end your prayer, say, "I believe it and receive it in Jesus' Name." Then choose to believe it and receive it.

TAKE ACTION
Write down some questions you can ask others in order to connect and relate to others.

_____

_____

_____

_____

_____

_____

_____

_____

_____

_____

_____

_____

_____

PRAY THE WORD
1 Corinthians 9:16-22, Thank You, Lord, for helping me to reach others for Jesus without compromising on Your Word. Thank You for giving me the words to speak and the questions to ask. When you pray, be sure pray in faith without doubting. When you end your prayer, say, "I believe it and receive it in Jesus' Name." Then choose to believe it and receive it.

Day 9: Get Back Up

For a righteous man may fall seven times and rise again.
Proverbs 24:16

DEVOTIONAL

"When champions fail, they get back up and try again. They don't let failure discourage them." Mary Ellen Clark

Just because we fail, it doesn't mean that our journey is over! The most important part of falling down is getting back up and learning from it!

I don't know if you have a perfectionistic tendency like I do, but it's something that I have had to overcome my whole life. If I failed or if I didn't do something "perfectly," I felt like I had to start over again. For example, today people compliment me all the time on how good my handwriting is and how it looked like I typed it up on a computer...well, there's a story for that. I was such a perfectionist. When I was in middle school all the way through college, anytime I would mess up when I was writing, even if it was when I was taking notes in class, I would go home and rewrite everything until it was perfect. If I messed up on one tiny letter, I would go back and rewrite the whole page. That was not great for my sanity, however, it did work well for helping me to study.

Having an attitude of perfection paralyzes you and it keeps you stuck. It's not a fun way to live and leads to a whole lot of stress. Perfectionism comes from a place of fear. It asks, "What if I mess up?" "What if I get it wrong?" "What if I'm not good enough?"

Job 3:25 tells us what happens when we allow ourselves to be controlled by fear. It says, "For the thing I greatly feared has come upon me, and what I dreaded has happened to me." If we know about the life of Job, we know that a lot of negative things happened: he lost his animals, he lost his servants, and he lost his children. Then, he got sick and had to deal with horrible skin sores. That's not where it ended. If it was, it would have been bad enough. Then, his friends came and visited him and were not very encouraging. In a time where Job is fighting to turn to God, his friends are pulling him down further. Needless to say, it was a tough time for Job.

Why did all of this happen? Because of his fear. His fear almost destroyed him. He let fear control him and it opened the door to the devil to work in his life. When we choose to stay in fear instead of faith, we are pushing away God and saying, "Sorry God, I don't want your protection." When we choose to stand in faith, on the Word of God, we are closing the door to the devil and allowing God's protection and safety take care of us.

But how do we stand in faith and not fear? Know that fear will try to creep into your life. That doesn't mean that what happened to Job is going to happen to you. However, if you do catch yourself start to feel fear or anxiety start to creep in, recognize it for what it is, go to God and talk to Him about it. Then, get in the Word and find verses on standing in faith and start to speak them and believe them.

CONNECT
Is there something that has been stressing you out or that you feel anxious or scared about? Or maybe there is an area of your life that you could just grow some more in your faith concerning that area. Take time today to talk to God about it. When you pray, be sure pray in faith without doubting. When you end your prayer, say, "I believe it and receive it in Jesus' Name." Then choose to believe it and receive it.

TAKE ACTION
Grab your Life Book, start a section on faith verses. Here are some verses that you can go to in order to stand in faith. Not sure what the Life Book is, be sure to go back to Part 2:

Dare to Be Confident, Day 6.

1. **Isaiah 26:3**-You will keep him in perfect peace, whose mind is stayed on You, because he trusts in You.

2. **Isaiah 41:10**-Fear not, for I am with you; be not dismayed, for I am your God. I will strengthen you, yes, I will help you, I will uphold you with My righteous right hand.

3. **Deuteronomy 31:6**- Be strong and of good courage, do not fear nor be afraid of them; for the Lord your God, He is the One who goes with you.

4. **Isaiah 12:2**-Behold, God is my salvation, I will trust and not be afraid; for Yah, the Lord, is my strength and song; He also has become my salvation.

5. **Psalm 118:6**-The Lord is on my side; I will not fear. What can man do to me?

6. **Luke 8:50**-But when Jesus heard it, He answered him saying, "Do not be afraid; only believe…"

PRAY THE WORD

Thank You, Lord that, Luke 8:50, that I will choose to not be afraid, but to put my trust in You and Your Word.

Day 10: Stand United

And if a house is divided against itself, that house cannot stand.
Mark 3:25

DEVOTIONAL

Has someone ever done something to you or someone else you know and it really bothered you? Like, you couldn't even stand being in the same room with that person because of it? I know I have.

I remember a time when a really good friend of mine all of a sudden stopped talking to me. I couldn't figure out what was going on and it really bothered me. She was someone I had considered one of my best friends. Since Matthew 18:15 tells us that, "If your brother offends you, go to them," that's exactly what I did. She told me that there was nothing wrong and that she was sorry that I felt that way. Things got better for a couple days before it went back to her not talking to me. It really bothered me, but at that point, I didn't have anything else I could do, but give it to God.

All was good; however, the truth eventually came out, as it always does. My friend was actually just using my friendship in order for her gain better friends. She knew that I knew a lot of people, so she was using me to get to them. The problem was, she had no real intention of being friends with me. I wouldn't have minded introducing her to my friends if she had asked. It hurt. So much so, that I honestly couldn't stand even being in the same room with her. I saw what she was doing and it continued to pull at my emotions. It wasn't until quite a few months later that I realized that I was holding offense toward her. Even though she had completely wronged me, I had made the choice to be offended. Now, I needed to make the choice to not stay in that offense, but to completely forgive her. I can pray for her, but I had to let that offense go and move on. I had to trust that God had a better plan in store for me.

The devil likes to use offense to attack us. He knows that, as Mark 3:25 says, a house divided against itself will fall and the enemy wants more than anything to see us fall. The good news, is we have a choice to not become offended. It's actually up to us to make that decision. If we choose to stay offended, it will eventually take us completely off of the will of God and it will end His blessings in our lives. If we choose to forgive, we choose to be free from those who hurt us and free to walk in God's blessings.

We will all have opportunities to get offended, but it's whether or not we choose it that makes a difference. So, what do we do when we start to get offended? How do we make the choice not to stay offended?

1.We start by evaluating what's really going on. The enemy wants us offended so that we fall. Then, take a step back and get with God. Talk to Him about what's going on and in that moment choose to praise Him because of His goodness. He will work everything out for your good. Psalm 61:2, "From the end of the earth I will cry to You, when my heart is overwhelmed; lead me to the rock that is higher than I."

2.Next, we need to make the choice to soak in God's love for us…not just that He loves us, but also how He loves us. John 3:16 tells us that God loved us so much that He sent His son to die for us so that we can have eternal life with Him. God knew all of the crazy things we would ever do in life and He still chose to love us and die for us anyway! God could have given up on us a long time ago, but because of how He loves us, He never would. He chooses to love without conditions.

3.Lastly, we need to make the choice to love those who have hurt us that same way God loves us, without conditions. That doesn't mean that we trust that person again right away. Trust is earned, but we can choose to love them. 1 John 2:10 tells us, "He who loves his brother abides in the light, and there is no cause for stumbling in him." That word, "stumbling" means "offense." When you choose to love others, even when it's hard, it's almost impossible to be offended.

CONNECT

Are you dealing with offense today? If so, take time to talk to God about it. If not, that's great. Go ahead, though, and ask God to help you see when offense tries to creep in, so you can overcome it immediately. When you pray, be sure pray in faith without doubting. When you end your prayer, say, "I believe it and receive it in Jesus' Name." Then choose to believe it and receive it.

TAKE ACTION

Create a new section in your Life Book with verses about offense. Write down the verses above to help you continue in freedom.

1. _____

_____

_____

_____

_____

2. _____

_____

_____

_____

_____

3. _____

_____

_____

_____

_____

PRAY THE WORD

Thank You, Lord, Romans 14:19, that I will make it a priority to live a life of peace with harmony in my relationships. I will eagerly seek to strengthen and encourage those around me.

Day 11: Cast Your Cares

Be anxious for nothing, but in everything by prayer and supplication, with thanksgiving, let your requests be made known to God; and the peace of God, which surpasses all understanding, will guard your hearts and minds through Christ Jesus.
Philippians 4:6-7

DEVOTIONAL

So many people today are either worried about something or stressed out. Whether it be school or something we heard in the news or something going on with our friends or our family, it's easy to fall into the trap of worry and anxiety.

Philippians 4:6 tells us to be anxious for nothing. I don't know about you, but that is a lot harder than it sounds. Sometimes I don't even realize that I am anxious or worried. It's so easy to get used to, however, Paul is telling us to be anxious for nothing. We don't have to worry about anything!

You may be thinking, "Is that even possible?" It is possible! God wouldn't tell us to do something that wasn't possible to do. How do we do this, though? How do we truly give it over to Him?

Philippians 4:6 goes on to say, but in everything by prayer and supplication, with thanksgiving, let your requests be made known to God. The word, "supplication" just implies that you take time with God alone and earnestly give over to him whatever is worrying you or getting you down.

The key to giving it to God is the very next part, "with thanksgiving." When we come to God, we don't need to come to Him from a soap box and tell Him everything is so wrong and complain. We can go to God from a position of victory over this area because Romans 8:37, we are more than conquerors. Being a conqueror is great because that means we go into the battle knowing that we are going to win. Being more than a conqueror, though, implies that when we go into battle, we know that the battle has already been won! Pray in faith, thanking God for that victory.

Then, as we give it over to God, that's when Philippians 4:7 takes place, "The peace of God, which surpasses all understanding, will guard our hearts and minds through Christ Jesus." It's a peace that we can't explain (it's a peace that conquers all chaos). We don't understand why we have peace when no-one else does.

However, when we give anything to God, we need to replace that with something else, otherwise we will fall right back into worry and anxiety. Philippians 4:8 tells us what we can replace those thoughts with. It says, "Finally brethren, whatever things are true, whatever things are noble, whatever things are just, whatever things are pure, whatever things are lovely, whatever things are of good report, if there is any virtue and if there is anything praiseworthy—meditate on these things."

So, whenever you feel worry or anxiety creeping in, find something you can thank God for, something good that's going on in your life and choose to think about that instead.

CONNECT
Take time to talk to God about anything that is weighing heavy on you...that could be school, family, something that's going on with a friend. Read Philippians 6 and choose to stand on God's Word concerning whatever is weighing on you. When you pray, be sure pray in faith without doubting. When you end your prayer, say, "I believe it and receive it in Jesus' Name." Then choose to believe it and receive it.

PRAY THE WORD
Thank You, Lord, that Philippians 4:6-7, I am making the choice to not be anxious, but instead I am choosing to turn to You with thanksgiving as I make my requests known to You.

Thank You, Lord, that the peace of God which surpasses all understanding is guarding my heart and mind through Christ Jesus.

Day 12: Seasoned with Salt

Walk in wisdom toward those who are outside,
redeeming the time. Let your speech always be with grace,
seasoned with salt, that you may know
how you ought to answer each one.
Colossians 4:5-6

WORD STUDY
TIME: Greek Word: kairos
Opportune time; set time; appointed time; proper time of action.

This isn't talking about the amount of time, but how we're using our time.

DEVOTIONAL

Foot in mouth syndrome. That was the story of my life. I grew up in a home where we learned to speak our mind no matter what....and the majority of the time when we did, it wasn't nice or pleasant.

Ephesians 4:15 says, "Let our lives lovingly express truth [in all things, speaking truly, dealing truly, living truly.] Enfolded in love, let us grow up in every way and in all things into Him Who is the Head, [even] Christ (the Messiah, the Anointed One).

See, I was really good at speaking the truth, I just had one little...okay, so maybe it wasn't so little...problem. I never learned how to speak the truth in love. For example, I remember sitting at a restaurant with a friend of mine when I was in college where we received the worst service I had ever had. Having worked at a restaurant myself, in my mind, this was not acceptable...and on top of the poor service, my server was training someone new. I remember telling my server that she was doing a poor job and I couldn't believe that her boss would have her of all people train someone.

Yeah...not so nice of me, right? It wasn't until I saw the look on my friend's face that that verse hit me square between the eyes. How am I supposed to shine the light of Jesus to those around me if I am not letting my life lovingly express the truth...note lovingly? I'm thankful that by God's grace, that was the last time and will be the last time I treated someone like that.

Colossians 4:5-6 tells us to walk in wisdom toward those who are outside...meaning people who haven't made Jesus the Lord of their life...so that we can make the most of every opportunity we have to shine the light of Jesus to them. It then goes on and says, "Let your speech always be with grace, seasoned with salt, that you may know how you ought to answer each one."

The lesson that I wished I had learned before that day is that my speech was always seasoned with grace. That it was life-giving and encouraging to the server and the girl she was training. I can't imagine how the server felt and that breaks my heart.

I encourage you to learn from the lesson I had to learn: that your words are always lifting others up and that they are seasoned with salt. That word salt is the same Greek word that is used for prudence. Prudence is simply a fancy word that means "wisdom that keeps us from future challenges."

CONNECT

Take time today to talk to God about your words. Are you shining the light of Jesus to those who are around you as you speak to them? Have you ever given thought to the words you are speaking? If not, ask God to help you become more aware of your words. When you pray, be sure pray in faith without doubting. When you end your prayer, say, "I believe it and receive it in Jesus' Name." Then choose to believe it and receive it.

TAKE ACTION

Intentionally go out of your way to encourage someone. Shine your light in a way that leaves them feeling encouraged. This isn't flattery...flattery is encouraging someone about something that's not true (for example: saying, "I love your shirt," when you really think it's ugly). Be truthful. Write below how you encouraged someone today and how it made you feel in return.

_____

_____

_____

_____

_____

_____

_____

_____

_____

_____

_____

_____

_____

_____

_____

PRAY THE WORD

Thank You, Lord, that Colossians 4:5-6, as I walk in wisdom toward those who don't know you, that I am making the most of every opportunity You have given me. I pray that my speech is always with grace, seasoned with salt, so that I am leaving others with a taste of Your goodness.

Day 13: Follow the Leader

For God did not send His Son into the world to condemn the world, but that the world through Him might be saved.
John 3:17

```
WORD STUDY
SAVED: Greek Word: sōzo

To Save: to deliver or protect; to heal; to preserve; be
made whole
```

DEVOTIONAL

When I think of someone who is a great leader, I think of someone who is tenacious. Someone who doesn't quit when things get hard. I think of someone who is honest and transparent...they are genuine and let you know that they were once right where I was. I think of someone who is passionate about their calling. Someone who is patient and kind. Someone who is creative and always looking for ways to make other people's lives better. I think of someone who listens to others and helps to give proper perspective in certain situations. I think of someone who is an encourager.

Jesus is an example of someone who is a strong leader. He was someone who transformed the lives of many people no matter where He went or what he was doing. In order for us to be a great leader, we can look at the life of Jesus and emulate what He did.

1. Jesus kept in mind His God-given purpose in every decision that He made. He knew that His purpose was to reunite us again with God and therefore He lived His life with that in mind. Hebrews 12:2 tells us that it was for the joy that was set before Him that He endured the cross. That joy that He set before Him was you and it was me. Jesus knew His purpose. He knew that every choice that

He would make would lead Him closer to that purpose or further away from it.

2. Jesus knew the difference between what was urgent and what was important. Just because something is urgent, doesn't mean that it has to be us that takes care of it. If we aren't careful, we can live our lives taking care of cleaning up other people's messes and miss the reason we are here. Just like Jesus, we need to keep our end goal in mind. Luke 10:38-42 tells us about a time when Jesus visited Mary and Martha. When we read the verses, we see that Martha was so caught up in the urgent that she almost missed what was most important. She was so busy making sure everything was perfect, that she was missing the point. Jesus didn't have very many days left on the earth and wanted to share with them His wisdom. So many times, it's the urgent things in our lives that distract us from our God-given purpose.

3. Jesus understood the importance of great communication. Jesus taught us that communication doesn't happen until the person that we are communicating with actually understands what we are trying to say. Jesus connected with those who were around Him. He asked them a lot of questions. Asking someone questions helps you get to know them, but also helps them to gauge where they are. Jesus was relatable without compromising. He would share stories with them to help them see what He was talking about. We can do the same, whether it's sharing our story or someone else's story. Lastly, He left people feeling encouraged. He spoke life into them.

4. Jesus was also really good at loving people. His whole ministry was about how He could serve others and build a relationship with them. In John 6:38, Jesus tells us the reason He is here, "For I have come down from heaven, not to do My own will, but the will of Him (God) who sent Me." What is the will of God? 1 Timothy 2:4 says that

143

God desires all men to be saved and to come to the knowledge of the truth." People are the ultimate reason God has given us a purpose.

CONNECT

Take time today to talk to God about today's devotion. What is something that is standing out to you today. He is excited to get to spend time with you. When you pray, be sure pray in faith without doubting. When you end your prayer, say, "I believe it and receive it in Jesus' Name." Then choose to believe it and receive it.

TAKE ACTION

Out of these four areas:

1. Keeping your vision in front of you

2. Knowing the difference between what's urgent and what's important-and choosing the right one

3. Communication

4. AND Loving people

Which one could you use strengthening? What is one thing you can do today to grow that area of your life. Write it down and how you will take action.

PRAY THE WORD

Thank You, Lord, 1 Timothy 2:4, that you help me to keep your purpose in front of me at all times so that others may come to know You as their Savior.

Day 14: It Starts with You

*Go therefore and make disciples of all nations,
baptizing them in the name of the Father and of the
Son and of the Holy Spirit, teaching them to observe all
things that I have commanded you; and lo, I am with you
always, even to the end of the age.*
Matthew 28:19-20

DEVOTIONAL

Have you ever lost something that was valuable to you? Maybe it was a piece of jewelry or your homework assignment that is due in your next class or maybe even just your keys? When I was in high school, a friend of mine gave me a necklace as a gift that was worth a lot of money. Growing up, I didn't have a lot of money, so this gift was probably the nicest thing I owned. And guess what…I lost it. Where did I lose it? In our huge yard of all places! I was wearing it while I was practicing soccer and when I finished, it was no longer hanging around my neck. I was all over our yard kicking my soccer ball around. Talk about panic!

When I realized that I lost it, I didn't just throw my hands in the air and say, "Oh well, no big deal." I frantically searched my whole yard walking up and down in lines…scouring every bit of it. Guess what? I actually found that necklace! It was quite a miracle in that big yard.

Did you know that this is the same way (well, minus the fear) that God searches for someone when He sees someone who has not yet accepted Him as their Lord. He sees the people He created as valuable. When they are wandering on their own without Him, it makes His heart sad. He wants more than anything to be in a relationship with all of the people He created.

Luke 15 shares three different parables of things that were lost and eventually found. Each of these parables truly

145

shows us the heart of our loving Father. In Luke 15:4-7, it talks about the parable of the lost sheep. It says, "What man of you, having a hundred sheep, if he loses one of them, does not leave the ninety-nine in the wilderness, and go after the one which is lost until he finds it? And when he has found it, he lays it on his shoulders, rejoicing. And when he comes home, he calls together his friends and neighbors, saying to them, 'Rejoice with me, for I have found my sheep which was lost!' I say to you that likewise there will be more joy in heaven over one sinner who repents than over ninety-nine just persons who need no repentance." I love seeing the heart of our Father.

Before leaving the earth, Mark 16:15 tells us Jesus' last words. He said, "Go into all the world and preach the gospel to every creature (person)." Since God desperately wants a relationship with His creation…us, it's important that we take these words to heart. God is saying, go into your world… wherever that would be (it could be school; or it could be the mall; or it could even mean leaving the country to go on a mission trip in a third world country) and share the Good News. What is the Good News? That God is not mad at them, but He's madly in love with them! What is your world? It's anywhere that you are…your circle of influence.

When sharing Jesus with others here at home, it's important to develop a relationship. I'm not saying make these people your best friend or hang out with them all the time. However, it's important to make a point to go out of our way to talk to them and encourage them in order to get to know them. The best way to share Jesus with someone who doesn't know Jesus is to just focus on getting to know the person we're talking to by asking them questions. Eventually, if we ask enough questions…maybe not all at the same time, but over time, we will hit a pain point in their life.

Pain points are usually an open door for sharing Jesus. When they share a pain point with you, this is a great time to show them that you can relate to them by sharing with them your story or a story of someone you know that has been where they are. After sharing the story, tell them what Jesus has done for you (or the person you are sharing the story about) and how He has helped turn that around. If they seem receptive, ask them, "Have you ever entered into a life-transforming relationship with Jesus?" It's important NOT to ask if they are a Christian. Being a Christian can be cultural for some people, because they were raised in a Christian family or used to go to church.

If they say no, let them know that God wants more than anything to heal their pain or maybe an emptiness inside of them, and He wants to have a relationship with them. God is standing with His arms wide open ready to receive them in. Then ask them, "Why not surrender your life to a loving Father, where you can find peace and joy and purpose? Would you like to start a life-transforming relationship with Jesus?"

If they are open to receiving Jesus, lead them in the prayer of salvation. More important than the words that are said are 4 important components to the prayer of salvation. These include:

1. **Repentance:** This word just means to turn from doing things their own way to deciding to go God's way. In Acts 17:30, God charges all men to repent—to change their mind and go His way.

2. **Belief in Jesus:** that He died for them and was raised from the dead. Romans 10:9-10 says, if you confess with your mouth that Jesus is Lord and believe in your heart that He was raised from the dead, you will be saved.

3. **Receiving Jesus as their Lord.**

4. **Saying, "Jesus is my Lord!"** Romans 10:13 says that everyone who calls upon the Name of the Lord will be saved.

Here is an example of a prayer of Salvation:

"Father, in Jesus' Name, I come to You. Sin and Satan, I turn my back on you. Jesus I turn to you now. Jesus, I believe that you died for me. Jesus, I believe that you were raised from the dead just for me. Come into my heart. Be my Lord. Today I am beginning a brand new relationship with you in Jesus' Name. Amen

Then ask them, "Can you tell me that Jesus is your Lord?" Make sure they say the actual words, "Jesus is my Lord." The reason this is so important is because in 1 Corinthians 12:3 says that no man can say, "Jesus is Lord," except by the Holy Spirit. If they have received Jesus, the Holy Spirit is on the inside of them.

CONNECT
Take time today to talk to God about who He would like you to share the Good News with. If it scares you to step out and lead someone to Jesus, talk to God about that, too. He loves getting to spend time with you and is walking with you every step of the way. When you pray, be sure pray in faith without doubting. When you end your prayer, say, "I believe it and receive it in Jesus' Name." Then choose to believe it and receive it.

TAKE ACTION
Ask God who He wants you to share the Good News with. When He talks to you about someone, step out and begin to talk to that person. Start by connecting with them, asking them questions, then sharing your story (or someone else's), and then asking them if they would like to start a relationship with Jesus.

_____

_____

_____

_____

_____

_____

_____

_____

_____

_____

_____

_____

_____

_____

_____

_____

_____

_____

_____

_____

_____

_____

_____

PRAY THE WORD

Thank You, Lord, that Matthew 28:19-20, I am choosing to take you up on Your commission. I will share the Good News with those who are around me. Thank You for always going with me.

Thank You!!

I want to start by thanking my Lord and best friend Jesus Christ for the ability to write this book. I was a mess before I met Jesus and yet He still decided to take me in, forgive me and make me new. It's because of Him that I have the honor of serving teens today.

Next, I want to thank my incredible family: my husband Ken who has always supported me and made me feel like a champion no matter what. Thank You! I love you so much! Also, thank you Chara and Javon for being the best kids a mom could ever have. You are a blessing to my life and I love you both!

Tom and Duonna Worstell, thank you! You were more than camp directors to me during my college years. You really showed me what it meant to live for Jesus. With you both, I had some of the most pivotal conversations that transformed my Christian journey.

Thank You, Pastor Rob and Abby Simms! It has been an honor to to serve teens with you both. You both have helped me to believe in myself when I had no confidence and showed me how to be a real leader. I am so excited for many more years with Real Joy!

Thank You, Pastor Jim and Mrs. Anne Frease! I thank God almost every day for the blessing and an honor it is to get to be a part of a church that teaches the true word of God and shows us how to make a big impact for Him. My life has been forever transformed by the Truth of the Word that you teach.

Thank You, Justin and Courtney Cappon for seeing the dreams that God placed in my heart and helping me to bring them to pass. I am blessed beyond belief that He has brought you all into my life.

Thank You, Ashli Townsend for allowing me to speak into your life. I cannot wait to see all that God is going to do through you! He has an incredible plan set out for your life.

Thank You, Paula Lautzenheiser for being like a sister to me. Thank You for taking the time to read through this devotional and helping me to make this dream happen. You are a blessing my friend.

Lastly, I want to thank all of you who have taken the time to read this devotional. I pray that it is a blessing to you and that it helps you walk out your relationship with God long and strong.

www.ingramcontent.com/pod-product-compliance
Lightning Source LLC
Chambersburg PA
CBHW071857020426
42331CB00010B/2558